QUASI-RELIGIONS

HUMANISM, MARXISM AND NATIONALISM

Quasi-Religions
Humanism, Marxism and Nationalism

JOHN E. SMITH

St. Martin's Press   New York

All rights reserved. For information, write:
Scholarly and Reference Division,
St. Martin's Press, Inc., 175 Fifth Avenue,
New York, N.Y. 10010

First published in the United States of America in 1994

Printed in Hong Kong

ISBN 0–312–12175–X

Library of Congress Cataloging-in-Publication Data applied for

Contents

'... the mutual relations of the religions proper are decisively influenced by the encounter of each of them with secularism, and one or more of the quasi-religions which are based on secularism.'

Paul Tillich

Series Editor's Preface

A series of monographs on themes in comparative religion might possibly give rise to misgivings in the minds of some readers because of misconceptions concerning the nature of comparative religion. It is often maintained, for example, that comparisons are odious; that religious comparisons are more odious than most; and that those who are concerned with comparative religion are only comparatively religious. The aim and purpose of this series of monographs, however, is not to present a comparatively religious outlook, nor to engage in odious comparisons which could result in one religious tradition being elevated to a position of superiority over others. The intention rather is to look at what might be called 'family resemblances' that pertain in the major religious traditions of the world.

Contributors to the series were asked to examine certain basic themes in the different world religions from an empathetic standpoint – that is, so far as possible, from within the religious traditions concerned and in a way that would meet with the approval of adherents of those religions. Since Christianity is the basic religious tradition of the West it was considered appropriate that the comparative thematic approach adopted by the series should involve Christianity on each occasion, and that religious themes in the different religious traditions of the world should be related to similar themes in the Christian tradition.

An indication of this approach would be the way in which the mystery of divinity takes different forms and finds expression in a variety of ways in different religious traditions. The Tetragrammaton or Logos of the Judeo-Christian tradition, for instance, might take the form of the Tao of the Chinese religious tradition, or the Brahman/Atman synthesis of the Hindu way of life, or the Kami of Shinto. A similar comparative approach involving 'family resemblances' would apply to other themes, such as creation and emanation; death and immortality; liberation and salvation; revelation and enlightenment; ethics and morality; the Kingdom of God, moksha and nirvana; and the ritual practices involved in the realisation of ultimate goals.

Naturally the choice of themes for the different monographs in the series, which include a comparison of the relation of Hinduism, Buddhism, Islam, Judaism, Japanese religions, Chinese religions, Sikhism, Zoroastrianism, primitive religions and Humanism with Christianity, would depend to a great extent on the way in which the different contributors to the series approached their subject matter. But the concept of empathy prevails throughout and the odious kinds of comparisons sometimes associated with comparative religion, albeit mistakenly, are excluded.

It is hoped that this open-ended thematic approach to comparative religion will prove helpful to the enquiring mind. In the pluralistic religious situation of today, with its great variety of religious experiences, we ought to be able to escape from the small island of our own culture, and from the ghetto mentality that would confine us to the insights of a single religious tradition. Such a mentality simply isolates us from the richness and diversity of other cultures and from the deep, spiritual insights of other religious traditions.

GLYN RICHARDS

1
The Religions Proper and Quasi-Religions

No serious discussion of religion, East or West, in relation to society and the contemporary world is possible without taking into account a distinction between *religion* understood as a pervasive dimension in human life and the world historical *religions* – such as Judaism, Islam, Christianity, Buddhism and Hinduism. These religions have defined themselves through their respective objects of worship, their religious communities, their sacred literatures, sacred persons, and their systems of morality. These particular religions represent historical traditions that, under individual cultural, political, geographical and other conditions, came into being as expressions of the human response to the sacred, the transcendent or whatever reality was regarded as Ultimate and worthy of an unconditional devotion. With respect to religion itself as a pervasive fact in human history, we must resist the nominalist tendency to say that 'religion' is merely a collective noun or name for these historical religions because that obscures the fact that religion is a distinctive dimension of human life and experience and that, as such, it is not exhausted in the particular religions that have appeared nor is it confined to the lives of those who adhere to these religions. Just as 'morality' is not identical with, nor merely a name for, the many ethical systems that have developed throughout the world, but the dimension of evaluation and appraisal of human conduct and the good life, religion likewise is not merely a name but an enduring facet of experience that concerns what is believed to be the reality on which human life and destiny ultimately depend. The importance of this truth about religion is that the concern it represents is not confined to those who have an affiliation with one of the historical religions, but is encountered in some way by everyone and, as we shall see, this fact is of great importance for understanding what I shall call 'quasi-religions'.

No one saw more clearly the ubiquity of the special concern to which religion answers than Paul Tillich. He expressed his conception of the nature of religion in many writings of which the following statement is typical. 'Religion,' he wrote

> is the state of being grasped by an ultimate concern, a concern which qualifies all other concerns as preliminary and which itself contains the answer to the question of the meaning of our life. Therefore this concern is unconditionally serious and shows a willingness to sacrifice any finite concern which is in conflict with it.[1]

Such a concern is the fundamental feature of the Western religions and means faith in and devotion to a supremely worshipful Being as expressed in the Jewish Bible, 'In the beginning, God . . .' and in the New Testament, 'In the beginning was the *Logos* . . .' and the first injunction is to love God with all one's heart, strength and mind and to reject all other gods as idols. Despite the enormous differences that exist between the Western religions – Judaism, Christianity and Islam – and those of the East, there are counterpart conceptions of God or the divine in the Hindu traditions and in some forms of Buddhism. In the *Bhagavad-Gita*, for example, Krishna is many times referred to specifically as 'God incarnate' and in the *Mahabharata*, Yudishthira who is the incarnation of the god Dharma – righteousness and justice – and who exists in tension with Krishna, acknowledges that he loves him because Krishna is God, the 'omniscient Creator and Ordainer' of all things.[2] In the Vedanta, moreover, even if it is not the heart of Hinduism that the *Gita* is, we find reference to two principles, matter and spirit and to God, a third principle, who is both and who 'impels to action'.[3] Even in Buddhism with its early 'atheistic' tendency, the Buddha comes to replace the God of Yoga as the object of worship as can be seen today in the Buddhist temples throughout South-East Asia. In all cases it is the nature of God as justice, mercy, righteousness and love that, like the famous plumbline of the Prophet Amos, provides the measure or standard for what human life should be and thus serves as the basis for diagnosing the human predicament and what there is wrong about the 'natural' man which separates him from that goal. It is in this connection that Tillich proposed that the understanding of the world religions and the quasi-religions is better accomplished by asking the question of the 'intrinsic aim of existence' or the *telos* of all things, than by comparing the different conceptions of God, man, history or salvation. He cites Plato's

vision of the *telos* of man as 'becoming similar to the god as much
as possible', and suggests an arresting comparison between Christianity and Buddhism as an example. In Christianity it is the *telos*
of 'every*one* and everything united in the Kingdom of God: in
Buddhism it is the *telos* of every*thing* and everyone united in the
Nirvana'.[4]

With this generic conception of religion as a background, one can
understand the acknowledged world religions – Judaism, Islam,
Christianity, Buddhism and Hinduism – as particular apprehensions of the religious reality, whether in theistic terms as in the
three Western religions, or in non-etheistic terms as in Buddhism
and in the monism of the Indian traditions. Though differing in
crucial respects from each other, they exhibit a common pattern
that makes it possible to compare them with each other. That
pattern, briefly stated, is threefold, starting with a *diagnosis* of the
human predicament based on the nature of the religious ultimate
aimed at locating what is wrong with our natural existence and
what separates us from an ideal fulfilment in God, or Nirvana or
the One. The apprehension of this separated or 'fallen' state of
humanity leads naturally to a *quest* for that reality which has the
power to overcome the flaw in our being disclosed in the diagnosis.
The quest is for a *deliverer* which overcomes the flaw and restores
the wholeness of our being. The deliverer in whatever form it may
take – the Torah of Jahweh, the Enlightenment of the Buddha, the
atoning work of Christ, the Insight concerning *Brahman* and *Atman*
in the Vedanta – is always the central focus of religious devotion
because of its power to bring release, salvation or deliverance from
the flaw in human existence revealed in the diagnosis.

The idea that there is any *general pattern* or structure of religion
manifested in the religions proper has often been denied, but
usually for the wrong reasons. This pattern as a generic structure is
not itself to be regarded as a religion, nor is it to be supposed that
appealing to such a pattern is a way of supporting the nonsensical
claim that all religions 'say the same thing'. On the contrary, the
common pattern is what enables us to say that these religions are
all concerned with the deliverance of human beings from evils
inherent in the human predicament and through comparison we
can see more clearly the *different* ways in which this predicament is
defined and the *different* ways in which it is believed to be overcome. Thus, far from blunting differences, appeal to the pattern
makes it possible to identify and understand them. Since, however,

students of the world religions have often expressed doubts about the existence of any common pattern in them, it is necessary to join the issue. Zaehner, in a paragraph from his book, *Concordant Discord*, which may seem at first to deny the existence of any generic pattern in religion, actually confirms it in one essential feature:

> It is then only too true that the basic principles of Eastern and Western, which in fact means Indian and Semitic, thought are, I will not say irreconcilably opposed; they are simply not starting with the same premises. *The only common ground is that the function of religion is to provide release*: there is no agreement at all as to what it is that man needs to be released from. The great religions are talking at cross purposes. (p. 324; italics added)

This 'common ground', however, is very important since it shows that what I have been calling the 'deliverer' or the means of being made whole again, is found in some form in all the religions. There need not be agreement among the religions about what man needs to be delivered from – what I have been calling the 'flaw' disclosed in diagnosis – or about the nature of the deliverer or the form of release, since the function of a generic structure of religion as such is to help us see the differences between religions and what they mean. What we need to grasp in all cases is what a given religion takes to be the chief obstacle standing in the way of human fulfilment and what it envisages as the means of release.

The point is that the world religions *are* dealing with the same *problem* and it comes into view when we see that in each case there is a beginning with a profound sense that there is something 'wrong' with our natural existence – in Judaism it is the 'heart of stone' that rebels against the divine Law; in Christianity it is the 'natural man' prone to sin in conflict with the 'spiritual man' – which is disclosed in a diagnosis made by comparing natural existence with a vision of redeemed life such as the Enlightenment that overcomes the suffering stemming from inordinate desire, the transformation of the heart of stone into a 'heart of flesh' where the Law is written in the 'inward parts', the coming into being of the spiritual man through the love of God as manifest in Christ. The cycle ends with the discovery of the deliverer, the means whereby the wrongness is overcome. Different as these religions are, there are *counterparts* in each of them for the elements in this pattern and these indicate that they are addressing the same underlying problem – What is the good life for human beings, what stands in the way of achieving it and what can overcome the obstacle? We may even go so far as to say that the very existence of religion itself as a generic trait in human life in the world is evidence that we are aware of being separated from or estranged from our essential nature.

Hence it is far too strong to say, as Zaehner does, that these religions are 'talking at cross purposes', since he admits that, despite the great difference between them, they have a common function. It is this function of release, in correlation with the diagnosis of what man is to be released from, that enables us to understand, for example, the point in comparing the dominant trend in Eastern religion where release is expressed in terms of being saved *from* the world with the emphasis in the West on transformation of the self *within* the world. Such a contrast makes sense precisely because of the common ground to be found in the generic structure of religion as it manifests itself. The very different conceptions of release, or, as I would prefer, the more inclusive term 'deliverance', take on new significance when we see that they represent different means for dealing with essentially the *same problem*, namely, how to overcome what prevents man from an envisioned ideal fulfilment. And, of course, the respective resolutions will themselves be functions of what I have called the diagnosis of the human predicament or the determination of what is wrong with natural existence and hence what needs to be conquered.

I suspect that what concerns Zaehner in his stressing 'not starting with the same premises', and speaking 'at cross purposes' in considering the world religions is something about which I am in total agreement, namely, his rejection of simplistic attempts to discuss Buddhism or Hinduism in terms of Christianity or to 'harmonise' the pronouncements of the different religions as if there were some underlying or hidden core that is supposed to unite them. That is simply false, but it is not entirely true, as Zaehner says, that 'they do not deal with the same subject-matter' (p. 439), since, as I have pointed out, these religions address the same underlying problem. If this were not so it would make no sense to discuss them in any relations to each other at all; the most that could be done would be to consider them one at a time in total isolation from each other and in that case it would not be possible for Zaehner to present them as he does through his illuminating thesis of 'concordant discord' which is itself a generic notion intended to throw light on the nature of religion as such. The philosophical error involved is as old as Nominalism, the belief that only individual and determinate realities exist and that whatever is general in character is to be found only in language. The usual way of expressing nominalism in the philosophy of religion, as we have seen (p. 1), is to say that 'religion' is only a collective name for particular religions and this obscures the fact that religion is a pervasive feature of human life in every culture and in every historical period. Hence there is no escape from the need to understand what religion is and means as a human concern that expresses itself, as Santayana said in a memorable phrase, 'under whatever sky . . .'

The concern expressed by Zaehner and others about the pitfalls encountered in what came to be known as 'comparative religion' is based on certain developments in that enterprise since it began in the early years of this century. William James in *The Varieties of Religious Experience* (1901) proposed that the proper role of philosophy *vis-à-vis* religion should not be what he considered as vain attempts to provide religion with metaphysical support, but rather with the development of a 'science of religions' by which he meant a description of generic features to be found in the world religions as distinct from specific beliefs and practices to be found in particular religious traditions.[5] I believe that his proposal was taken up in the form of the comparative study of religions and in its earlier days this discipline tended in the direction of 'harmonising' religious beliefs, sometimes working on the naive assumption that there is some level at which all religions 'really say the same thing'. That, of course, is nonsense, but it did lead to the sort of interpretation that Zaehner rightly criticises when he insists that the world religions are talking at cross-purposes or do not have the same subject matter. Recent developments since the time of Zaehner's Gifford Lectures (1967–9) have drastically changed the picture. There is a new dialogue between representatives of the major religions which is not concerned at all with 'harmonising' things, but instead aims at finding out, as far as this is humanly possible across cultures, what those in other cultures are expressing in their religious beliefs and practices. In short, there is now a serious attempt at communication where the aim is *not* to see other religions solely in terms of one's own, but to try to cross the bridge and catch the view from the other side. Essential, however, to this endeavour is the belief that what is under discussion is *religion*, that all participants in the dialogue are considering a pervasive dimension of human life wherever it is lived and hence that, despite differences, paradoxes, anomalies and contradictions, there is a continuity of concern that serves to identify the focus of the discussion.

What most needs to be emphasised about this pattern or structure of the world religions that are recognised as such, is that in every case the religious ultimate is not identical with any *finite* reality. This fact becomes clearly apparent in the struggle to be found in all these religions against idolatry, a struggle against the setting up of any conditioned thing or feature of ourselves and the world as ultimate in the sense that it would replace the religious reality.

We can approach the task of making clear what is meant by 'quasi-religions' by drawing a contrast between the religions proper and Humanism, Marxism, Nationalism and similar movements which have evoked loyalty and devotion in many parts of the world. The first and most obvious contrast is found in the fact that the ideal or the reality which forms the focus of loyalty and commitment in a quasi-religion is something that is finite and conditioned, an object among others drawn from experience of ourselves and the world. Humanism in its many forms has for its central concern human beings as such, although this concern is sometimes expressed in terms of mankind or an ideal human nature. From this perspective any reference to a transcendent reality is excluded; the horizon of Humanism is essentially naturalistic and is confined to human beings and the world open to human experience. Much more, of course, remains to be said about Humanism, but that must be postponed in order to draw the comparison with the world religions on this one point. The same holds true in the cases of Marxism and Nationalism.

Marxism both as the philosophical outlook expressed in Marx's writings and its political embodiment in Communist regimes is complex and presents more than one central concern or focus. One might point to the ideal of the classless society, to the overcoming of human alienation, to the dialectic of history and the overthrow of capitalism, or to the attack on religion as motivating concerns which have evoked intense loyalty and devotion from the masses in many countries. As with Humanism, these central concerns are all finite and conditioned and are derived from the social and political dimensions of human life. Not only is there no place for a transcendent reality, but in Marxism both theoretically and practically there is an avowed rejection of religion on the grounds that it offers a false picture of the human being and leads to alienation by holding up the vision of another world which distracts us from engaging in the radical criticism and transformation of the existing world.

Nationalism also has had many forms, but its central concern remains one and the same – the state or nation, whether in its actual form or in some idealised conception of its destiny, is set up as the ultimate object of loyalty and devotion. As we shall see, Nationalism as a quasi-religion goes far beyond the national self-consciousness that is the legitimate source of the unity and identity of a people and makes absolute claims for the superiority of a nation *vis-à-vis* other nations in the world arena, just as it makes similar demands on the citizens of the country to make the power and honour of the state their ultimate loyalty. We find the same pattern in the three quasi-religions to be considered; a particular reality that is finite and conditioned has been absolutised as the object of a loyalty that has no limits and acknowledges no loyalty higher than itself.

An important, if not the decisive, factor in the rise of quasi-religions has been those developments over the past century or more that are usually referred to as secularism or the secularisation of modern life. The growth of modern technological society and mass production, the rise of power politics and national ideologies, the creation of multinational corporations and international trade, the struggles between nations for power and prestige and within nations for justice and civil rights, plus many other features of contemporary society, have conspired to create a powerful and largely secular society in which the concerns of traditional religion have been submerged, and, in many cases, actively opposed as outmoded relics of the past. To see the extent of the change that has taken place one need only compare the hectic, frantic and often aimless character of contemporary life in cities large and small with life in the New England of the eighteenth century at the time of Jonathan Edwards. Although Puritan piety was losing ground at the time, the *whole* of life and human activities were still seen in relation to God and the destiny of the soul. Decisions and actions, the relations between people and the welfare of the community stood under the guidance of religious principles; there was time for meditation and reflection about the things that matter most and while, in a realistic view, there was evil and corruption, life was not exhausted in the all-consuming quest for money and power. At present there is scarcely any time left for such meditation or reflection about who and why we are. Thus there has been created a kind of secular 'void' in which a sense of lost meaningfulness prevails.

Such a void has had much to do with the development of quasi-religions; the concern for an ultimate object of devotion, a ground and standpoint for understanding and appraising all that we think and do, belongs essentially to being human and is not confined to those who have already committed themselves to an historic religious tradition. The human need for the fulfilment of that concern can be found in secular ultimates which function in human life in much the same way as the religious ultimates of the world religions and this is one of the reasons why it is legitimate to characterise the quasi-religions as belonging to religion.[6]

We must not, however, overlook another factor that has led to the formation and growth of quasi-religions and that is the failure of established religion to keep pace with change and to sustain relations of relevance to the contemporary situation. Such failure has come about in a number of ways. Religious traditions tend to regard their central message as timeless, but if this conception leads them to overlook the fact that the people and the culture they address are in time and are affected by change and that this demands continuing reinterpretation in each new period, they ossify and become ineffective. The religions have often lost credibility because of failure to take account of new knowledge about the world and human beings or, worse, because they have sought to encapsulate themselves within a stronghold of faith by adopting an anti-intellectualist stance that drives a wedge between reason and faith. The religions have often lost their prophetic or critical voice and have lent support to corrupt and oppressive regimes. Too much time has been spent contemplating the glories of the lilies of the field, while the fact that there are thieves (some of whom are in the churches) who steal, has been ignored.

These and other shortcomings have served to alienate the secular mind from religion in what used to be called its 'organized' form and have led it to look elsewhere for an object of devotion, something to be believed in which makes life worthwhile. The quasi-religions seen against this background become very attractive to those thus alienated, and this explains why these religions express hostility towards the established religions, regarding them as an evil to be overcome. As Tillich has pointed out, 'the main characteristic of the present encounter of the world religions is their encounter with the quasi-religions of our time'. He calls the situation paradoxical, and continues, 'Even the mutual relations of the religions proper are decisively influenced by the encounter of each of them with secularism, and one or more of the quasi-religions which are based on secularism.'[7]

The more detailed account of the quasi-religions presented in the chapters to follow will attempt to determine whether there is to be found in them counterparts to the features previously described as the common pattern or structure of the religions proper. Is there a counterpart to the diagnosis of the human predicament and a re-cognition of some basic flaw in human nature that needs to be overcome? Is there a counterpart for an ultimate reality? Is there a counterpart to faith and is there a counterpart to worship or venera-tion? The answer to these and other questions will help to make clear what justification there is for regarding the quasi-religions as 'religions' and also what is lacking in them even if they do respond to the human religious need.

There is one feature of the diagnosis to be found in the world religions which is more important than any other, and that is the emphasis placed on the deep-seated or *inherent* character attributed to what is believed to be the flaw in human beings which needs to be surmounted. This deficiency is seen as belonging to the structure of human existence and hence as an obstacle that is recalcitrant in the sense that it is not to be overcome by human effort alone. The Buddha, for example, in his quest for Enlightenment, broke with the cosmic consciousness of his native Hindu tradition and found the universal cause of suffering in a lack of true insight coupled with an inordinate desire or craving for evanescent things. This he regarded not as an accidental fact about the nature of life, but as an essential feature of its structure. The craving and the suffering belong to the life that has not yet been enlightened and the over-coming of both is not a matter of wish or will, but of a rigorous discipline aimed at providing limits and an orientation for an in-herent desire that would otherwise be without bounds. There are, to be sure, many forms of Buddhism, including that of so-called 'early' Buddhism, which claim that the goal reached by the Buddha can be achieved by any individual on his or her own by following the regimen of transformation outlined in the Path. This form, however, is not the only one and most other forms stress the im-possibility of reaching nirvana through human effort alone.

The intractable character of the flaw is even more prominent in the Western religions where the belief is that the being who has the flaw is not capable of overcoming it without resources from beyond the self. The importance of this point has often been overlooked.

The Western religions are 'realistic' in orientation; they take seriously the *actual* human situation as they conceive it and recognise the fact that it is with the 'unredeemed' person that we must deal and they do not suppose that this person *already has* the resources that are available only *after* redemption has taken place. The point can be effectively seen even in the case of a quasi-religion such as Marxism. Marx clearly had a conception of an ideal form of human existence – the new man in the classless society – but he also had a clear idea of *actual* man, the being of alienation in all its forms. Marx knew, even if many Marxists do not, that it was with this *alienated* man with all his deficiencies that he had to deal and that he could not appeal to the new man as if he were already a reality.[8] The underlying question is whether the being who is actually in need of transformation can accomplish the change required solely from present resources? The religions proper deny this possibility, largely because the flaw they see in the human creature is at the root of its being and infects all thought and conduct. The quasi-religions on the contrary find the obstacles standing in the way of human fulfilment to be of a less radical nature and view them as evils or problems which are manageable and to be dealt with through purely human powers.

It is essential at the outset to pose and try to resolve a problem which has led to considerable fruitless discussion in the past, namely, whether such movements as Humanism, Marxism and Nationalism are to be regarded as forms of 'religion'. Corliss Lamont, for example, in his learned and well thought out description of a Humanism that has gained wide acceptance, develops naturalistic Humanism as a philosophy and he clearly does not want to have it taken as a religion; for him, religion is inextricably tied to a belief in the supernatural which his Humanism excludes. In fact, he criticises those *religious* Humanists, largely Unitarian ministers, who signed the Humanist Manifesto of 1933 written by Roy Wood Sellars which opposed supernaturalism; Lamont writes, 'I feel that they need to justify more adequately than they have yet done their retention of the ancient and hallowed word *religion*.'[9] Further testimony in the same direction is to be found in the theme of a recent Conference sponsored by *Free Inquiry*, 'Living Without Religion; The Ethics of Humanism'.[10] It seems clear that these Humanists are strongly opposed to any identification of their position as a religion.

In the case of Marxism the situation is even clearer since there religion, usually identified with superstition, is a central focus of attack on the ground that it represents the supreme form of human alienation and oppression and thus stands in the way of the realisation of Marxist goals for society. Nationalism, by contrast, presents a far more complex picture since it has taken so many forms and is represented by national leaders, who, in turn represent various claims in behalf of the nations they command.

The important point is to avoid becoming involved in an un-illuminating argument in which the term 'religion' is tossed back and forth like a football between those who do not want to be so classified, on the one hand, and those who, on the other, are over-zealous in wanting to see such movements as we have been considering dubbed 'religions'. Sidney Hook, for example, repeatedly attacked Tillich's characterisation of religion in terms of 'ultimate concern' as an instance of what he called 'conversion by definition', and insisted that there was nothing religious about the naturalistic Humanism he espoused. At the other end of the spectrum there is Russell's attempt to express Marxism as a 'religion' by correlating it with the Judeo-Christian religious framework:

Yahweh = Dialectical Materialism
The Messiah = Marx
The Elect = The Proletariat
The Church = The Communist Party
The Second Coming = The Revolution
Hell = Punishment of the Capitalists
The Millennium = The Communist Commonwealth[11]

In order to avoid this see-saw of denial and ascription, I appeal to the concept of a 'quasi-religion' as a means of identifying and describing movements that have some similarity in structure and in the function they manifest in human life to the *religions proper*, i.e., to those historical traditions about which there is no argument that they are religions.

'Quasi-religion' is not a term of opprobrium nor does it imply any sort of negative judgement about these movements; it is meant to be as close to the purely descriptive as one may hope to get. I reject the expression that has sometimes been used in this connection – 'pseudo-religion' – because I believe it is both unfair and misleading, it suggests something counterfeit and implies that there is nothing of value in these substitute visions of human life. There are at least two closely related reasons for speaking of quasi-religions as movements having similarities in structure and function with the recognised religions; first, is the fact that many quasi-religions have been born out of the failures of the established religions to adjust to change and to recognise the need to reinterpret their traditions anew in each generation, if they are to retain the devotion of their adherents, and, second, the strong sense present among the followers of these secular movements that they are meant to provide a source of significance and purpose in human life and a general pattern of behaviour as a guide. The latter point is acknowledged quite explicitly by Lamont when he writes, referring to 'traditional religion', 'At its best it has given to [people] the opportunity of losing themselves in something greater than any individual and of finding themselves thereby in consecration to an ideal. This historic function of religion any present philosophy worthy of the name must fulfil.'[12] And since he is presenting Humanism as a philosophy it must be understood as intending to perform this religious function. Hence, in view of this admission, Humanism, even when set forth as a philosophy, is justifiably to be called a quasi-religion.

There is no doubt that the existence of evils rightly attributed to religious institutions and the clergy – suppression of free thought, acquiescence in the face of injustice, intolerance and fanaticism – has been a powerful factor behind the formation of quasi-religions, and explains their tendency to take an anti-religious stance. To maintain the self-criticism necessary if one is to avoid ideology and the absolutising of one's own position is very difficult in any situation, but it is especially difficult in the case of the positive religions where a message believed to have a divine sanction is involved. It is important to notice that the exposure of these evils associated with religions and the protest against them has not always come from hostile critics standing outside these religions. Biblical religion has a prophetic as well as a priestly side and some of the most severe criticism of religious beliefs and practices has come from men and women whose faith in the traditions they would purify is unquestioned. Paul Tillich understood the problem very well when he set forth what he called the 'Protestant Principle' according to which religious institutions must see themselves not only as dispensers of divine judgement but as subject to and not exempt from that same judgement. Reinhold Niebuhr made, from a religious standpoint, penetrating analyses of the 'ideological taint' not only in religion but throughout society, political life and world history, which masks the human self-interest and pretension often lurking behind the profession of lofty ideals. It is far easier to criticise an institution one is not identified with than to engage in self-criticism and this is one of the pitfalls confronting quasi-religions, especially when they are motivated by an anti-religious bias. The belief, for example, that a movement has the aim of dispelling religious illusions in the name of science, reason or sober truth is no guarantee that those engaged in such movements are without illusions of their own. No individual or institution is *actually* as good as the high ideals they espouse.

2

Humanism as a Quasi-Religion

Humanism has had many meanings and has assumed a great many forms throughout the world from the time of the fifth-century Greek philosopher Protagoras who proclaimed that 'Man is the measure of all things', through the Humanism of the European renaissance of the fourteenth-century and its ideal of the universal man, to the Humanist associations of the present. There have also been Humanisms within religious traditions, for example, some Unitarians and Universalists have shown considerable sympathy with the tenets of Humanism, and Jacques Maritain, the Catholic philosopher, developed what he called an Integral Humanism based on the thought of Thomas Aquinas and his interpreter John of St Thomas. These positions, however, would not be correctly described as quasi-religions. Given the protean form of Humanism, it is necessary to be very selective. The best statement that has been given of a naturalistic Humanism in the first half of this century is that of Corliss Lamont in his book previously referred to *Humanism as a Philosophy*, and, in view of its influence and the many historic sources said to have contributed to this form of Humanism, we may safely take it as an authoritative guide. In order to follow the further development of the movement for which Lamont speaks, we shall have recourse to a collection of essays, *The Humanist Alternative*, in which some thirty contributors from England, France, India and the Netherlands as well as America seek to make clear the meaning of Humanism.[1]

As a preliminary to setting forth the main contentions of Humanism, Lamont offers a brief statement of the contribution of philosophy as such to human life. Philosophy, he says, enables human beings 'to find significance in their lives, to integrate their personalities around some clear, consistent and compelling view of existence' (p.8). And he insists, as did William James, that everyone has some view of this sort, whether conscious or not. Humanism, he describes as the organisation into a consistent and intelligible whole 'the chief elements of philosophic truth that it can find in the past and present' (p. 19). The result of this gathering of insights is said to be summed up in eight central propositions; we shall attend to them in order.[2]

First, Humanism believes in a naturalistic cosmology or metaphysics or attitude towards the universe that rules out all forms of the supernatural and that regards Nature as the totality of being and as a constantly changing system of events which exists independently of any mind or consciousness.

Three points are noteworthy in this affirmation; first, that Nature with a capital 'N' – is the name for all that really is; second, that it is explicitly meant to exclude what are taken to be the 'supernatural' elements involved in religion; third, that Nature is independent of mind or consciousness, a view meant to represent realism or, as Sellars and Montague were willing to say, 'materialism', but in any case a view that excludes idealism in any form. Here Humanism is defined negatively by contrast with the supernatural.

Second, Humanism draws especially on the proven facts of science, and believes that man is an evolutionary product of this great Nature of which he is a part and that he is an inseparable unity of body and personality having no individual survival beyond death.

There is little need for comment on this proposition, beyond noting a second instance where Humanism is defined negatively by contrast with the idea of immortality supposed to be a fixed tenet of religions, and the use of the term 'personality' instead of mind.

Third, Humanism believes that human thinking is as natural as walking or breathing, that it is indivisibly conjoined with the functioning of the brain, and that ideas, far from existing independently in some separate realm, arise and have reality only when a complex human organism is interacting with its environment and is intellectually active.

The thrust of this proposition is against the over-emphasis in modern philosophy on knowledge itself as the key to understanding reality and some of the *idealisms* that have been developed from this standpoint.

Fourth, Humanism believes that mankind has the power and potentiality of solving its own problems successfully, relying primarily on reason and scientific method to do so and to enlarge continually his knowledge of the truth.

This proposition expresses a basic faith in mankind, in the capacity of science and philosophy to resolve the problems confronting human beings in the world and a hint of progressivism with respect to a continual enlargement of knowledge. The statement is slightly less strong than one quoted with approval earlier on proposing different ways of defining Humanism. '[Humanism] may be a philosophy of which man is the centre and sanction' (p. 18).

Fifth, Humanism believes, in opposition to all theories of universal pre-destination, determinism or fatalism, that human beings possess true freedom of creative action and are, within reasonable limits, the masters of their own destiny.

No comment is needed on this proposition; it is self-explanatory. The reference, however, to 'destiny' is noteworthy since, even if it be given a naturalistic meaning, the term has figured largely in all the world religions.

Sixth, Humanism believes in an ethics or morality that grounds all human values in this-earthly experiences and relationships; and that holds as its highest loyalty the this-worldly happiness, freedom and progress – economic, cultural and ethical – of all mankind, irrespective of nation, race or religion.

The main operative idea in this proposition is that morality is to have no basis in religion.

Seventh, Humanism believes in the widest possible development of art and of the awareness of beauty, including the appreciation of external Nature, so that the aesthetic experience may become a pervasive reality in the life of men.

This statement is a brief summary of the view presented by Dewey in *Art as Experience* where he sought to broaden the aesthetic dimension of experience and, so to speak, to bring art out of the confines of the museum.

Eighth, Humanism believes in a far-reaching social programme that stands for the establishment throughout the world of democracy and peace on the foundations of a flourishing and cooperative order, both national and international.

In referring to these eight points as a whole, Lamont offers a very
helpful summary; he writes,

> This philosophy can be more explicitly characterized as scientific
> Humanism, materialistic Humanism or democratic Humanism,
> depending on the emphasis that one wishes to give. Whatever it
> be called, Humanism is the viewpoint that men have but one life
> to lead and should make the most of it in terms of creative work
> and happiness; that human happiness is its own justification and
> requires no sanction or support from supernatural sources; that
> in any case the supernatural, usually conceived of in the form of
> heavenly gods or immortal heavens, does not exist; and that
> human beings, using their own intelligence and cooperating liber-
> ally with one another, can build an enduring citadel of peace and
> beauty upon this earth. (p. 21)

To this we should add the almost apocalyptic vision with which the
book closes:

> Despite the appalling world wars and other ordeals through
> which humanity has been compelled to pass during the first half
> of the twentieth century, I believe firmly that man, who has
> shown himself to be a very tough animal, has the best part of his
> career still before him. And there is at least the possibility that
> within the next few decades and before the close of this century
> the human race will emerge onto the lofty plateau of a world-
> wide Humanist civilization. (p. 349)

I shall refer to this statement later on in the discussion about the
status of Humanism as a quasi-religion.

Before going on to some later expressions of opinion about
Humanism and the changing conditions – historical, religious,
social, economic – to which Humanists want to respond, it will
prove illuminating to review the sources in philosophy, religion
and culture of the Humanism set forth by Lamont, in order to make
more concrete the propositions which make up his manifesto.

Socrates is clearly a source of great inspiration for Humanism,
especially his well known claim that the unexamined life is not
worth living, but also his claim that 'No harm can come to a good
man.' Lamont sees Socrates as the ideal martyr to truth in philosophy, the counterpart of Jesus as the religious martyr. And, of

course, Socrates's refusal to fear death is very important for Humanism since it aims both to emphasise that death is not to be dreaded as mysterious but is 'natural' and belongs to life, and to expose the illusion of immortality which is taken along with the supernatural, as the hallmark of all religion. Other philosophers in the ancient world, Epicurus, Democritus, Lucretius are said to belong to the Humanist tradition because of their naturalism or even materialism with their this-worldly emphasis and opposition to super-naturalism. Although Humanism eschews traditional religion, it does not hesitate to borrow from the insights of religious figures and the ideas to be found in religious literature which it finds congenial. Thus Buddha, Confucius and Jesus, according to Lamont, made significant contributions to Humanism, even if some of them were of a negative sort. The Buddha and Confucius are cited because of their disbelief in 'supernaturalism in the sense of the existence of a personal God and personal immortality' (p. 62). Buddha, Lamont claims, would have been horrified 'to find himself elevated to the status of a Divinity' and worshipped in the form of stone and metal statues, since his emphasis, as evidenced by the Noble Eightfold Path, was mainly on a code of conduct 'for this world' (p. 63), Confucius is likewise commended for having an ethical system aimed at happiness in the here and now and, as regards any life beyond the world, he is credited with saying, 'While you do not know life, what can you know about death?' (ibid.).

In addition, Lamont calls attention to the writings in the Jewish Bible – *Proverbs, The Song of Solomon* and *Ecclesiastes* – in which there is to be found, despite Hebraic supernaturalism, values attainable in this life which 'can stand up independently of sanctions or revelations from on high' (p. 64). He finds that the central theme in these books is the advice to enjoy life while it is possible, even though all achievement is transient and ultimately in vain.

The sayings attributed to Jesus are said to have much to offer any humane philosophy. 'Jesus', says Lamont, 'raised his voice again and again on behalf of Humanist ideals, such as the spread of altruism, the brotherhood of man, and peace on earth' (p. 66). There are, moreover, particular sayings which can be given a this-worldly interpretation consonant with Humanist teaching – 'Ye shall know the truth, and the truth shall make you free'; 'I am come that they might have life, and that they might have it more abundantly' (pp. 66–7). 'Humanism', Lamont concludes, 'holds that certain of

the teachings of Jesus possess an ethical import that will always be
pertinent for the human race; and that the Jesus portrayed by the
gospels represents one of the supreme personalities of all history'
(p. 67). In order to re-enforce the purely human side of Jesus,
Lamont offers a brief sketch of anti-Trinitarian thinkers from Arius
who attacked the Nicene Creed to Michael Servetus whose work
On the Errors of the Trinity was banned by Catholics and Protestants
alike, and on to modern day Unitarianism whose heroes include
William Ellery Channing, Theodore Parker and Emerson.

The broad sweep of this Humanism becomes clear when we are
told that Enlightenment Deism 'strengthened the secular, Humanist trends of the modern era, since it implied that men should
depend on their own efforts and intelligence . . . and not fall back
on a Divine Being' (p. 71). The Quakers, especially the Hicksite
wing, made their contribution to Humanism in their repudiation of
the Trinity, their philanthropic spirit and their stand against slavery.
Lamont states the general principle behind this eclecticism in terms
of the alleviation of human suffering and the extension of human
happiness upon this earth. Speaking of the world religions as such,
Lamont writes, 'Philosophical Humanists, while continuing to dis-
agree with supernaturalism in whatever guise it appears, welcome
as allies on specific economic, social and ethical issues all super-
naturalists who sincerely agree with them on such issues' (p. 74).

In addition to what Humanism finds congenial in both philosophy and religion, it also lays claim to many of the cultural resources
of Western civilization from the Athens of Pericles to the literary
realism of Theodore Dreiser and Carl Sandburg in America. Again,
the criterion for genuine Humanism is the setting up of human
accomplishment 'as the chief end of man' (p. 77). Thus Sophocles is
commended for writing:

> Many are the wonders of the world
> And none so wonderful as Man

Erasmus is noted for his opposition to other-worldliness, expressed
in the lines:

> . . . Drink deep, live long, be jolly,
> Ye illustrious votaries of folly

Shakespeare is important for supposedly omitting religion altogether, and Lamont points to the 'penetrating essay' of Santayana, 'The Absence of Religion in Shakespeare', and praises as

'one of the most memorable Humanist perorations' the lines from
Hamlet, 'What a piece of work is Man! How noble in reason! How
infinite in faculties' (p. 83). Voltaire and the French encyclopaedists
voiced the ideals of Humanism, although the former lapsed somewhat in his declaration that 'If there were no God, it would be
necessary to invent him.' The works of Alexander Pope, of Blake, of
Shelley along with those of Goethe and Schiller, and the music of
Beethoven are all said to be expressions of the values that make up
Humanism. The list could be expanded and to be included in it one
must deny God and the supernatural and join in some form of the
chorus, 'Glory to man in the highest, for he is the master of things'.

The full thrust of Lamont's Humanism is best seen in his chapter,
'This Life is All and Enough'. There great emphasis falls on assert-
ing the unity of body and personality (the latter is sometimes called
'mind') as demonstrated by 'science' so that just as the body and
personality live together and grow together, they die together. 'The
issue of mortality versus immortality is crucial', he writes, 'in the
argument of Humanism against supernaturalism' (p. 101). For
Lamont there is an indissoluble connection between the human
desire for a future life and belief in a Divine Being who can bring
this about. Hence it is essential that he insist, against all dualisms,
on the dependence of mind upon body and the extinction of both
upon death. He even invokes the Christian idea of resurrection as
reinforcing 'a close and indissoluble union between body and personality' (p. 118) and this is correct, but he fails to see that this is
one of the chief reasons why the classical Christian doctrine is *not*,
as Lamont supposes throughout, that of immortality – a mind
surviving without a body – but of Eternal Life expressed in Pauline
language, 'It is sown a *natural* body, and raised a *spiritual* body.'[3]
Neither for Judaism nor for Christianity is the human person
thought to be disembodied.

As might be expected, another of Lamont's targets in his cam-
paign against immortality is the cult of the Spiritualists and their
belief in communication with the dead who are on 'the other side'.
Sir Oliver Lodge, who claimed to have had messages from his dead
son, succeeded in gaining considerable notoriety for what was
called at the turn of the century, 'Psychic Research'. What intrigued
William James, at least for a time, and repels Lamont is the 'scientific' aura that surrounded Spiritualism. Continued existence beyond death, it was claimed, is not a matter of blind faith or a mere
hope, but a matter of experimental evidence. The difficulty, of

course, is that this 'evidence' seemed to be available only to firmly convinced Spiritualists. 'The emotional consequences of death', Lamont observes, 'have been so profound that discussion of the subject has rarely been carried on in an atmosphere conducive to unbiased conclusions' (p. 129).

Lamont moves on to what is his main concern, namely to deny that death is either evil or mysterious. 'Death', he says, 'in and of itself, as a phenomenon of Nature, is not an evil' (ibid.). Death, he continues, is not only altogether natural, but it has played a useful and necessary role in the course of biological evolution. Since, moreover, immortality is a vain conceit, death does away not only with paradises beyond life, but also with all threats of hell and purgatories. The Humanist response to death is 'to recognize the true meaning of death as the conclusion of our personal careers and to look it in the face with dignity and calm' (p. 132).

Humanism places the destiny of man 'within the very broad limits of this natural world' (p. 134), and the death of individuals 'cannot defeat the ongoing life of the nation or of humanity as a whole' (p. 135). This life is not only an opportunity for self-enjoyment; it is as well an opportunity to contribute significantly to more lasting human values, and 'to leave a name behind us that will be honored and beloved by the community' (pp. 135–6). This faith in the continuation of mankind through a progressive development of increasing control over nature to be brought about by scientific knowledge depends on the earth's remaining a habitable abode.

Here Lamont finds that his opponents are not theologians eagerly awaiting the Day of Judgement, but 'pessimistic scientists' claiming that the earth will some day become uninhabitable, 'all the living creatures upon it being extinguished' (p. 138).[4] Like Prometheus shouting defiance at Zeus his tormentor, Lamont declares, 'What I want to deny emphatically is the necessity of any ultimate doom for man' (ibid.). Actually, this statement is not as strong as it appears, since the main force of the denial, though it clearly involves the destiny of mankind, is directed against the idea that such doom is *necessary* and stems from Lamont's general rejection of necessitarianism.

The discussion moves on to Humanism's theory of the universe and man's place within it. The central thesis is that 'Nature itself constitutes the sum total of reality' (p. 145) and hence that the denial of the supernatural means both that there are no immortal souls and that the cosmos does not 'possess a supernatural and eternal God' (ibid.).[5] The vastness of the cosmos with its many galaxies disclosed by science leads Lamont to conclude 'that the universe at large is indifferent, *neutral* toward the welfare, the ideals and the fate of man' (p. 149). There is, moreover, no need for a First Cause behind the material universe and hence cosmological arguments for the existence of God are futile. Lamont, however, does take into account the infinite regress upon which these arguments depend. 'The fact is', he writes, 'that regardless of how far we push our inquiries, at one point or another we are compelled to assume *something self-existent* that possesses certain powers and potentialities' (p. 154). The solution is to accept the opinion of Aristotle 'that the universe is eternal' (ibid.). In addition, if we employ the principle of simplicity, or 'Ockham's razor', God turns out to be superfluous. At most, God and immortality 'symbolise' ethical values.

In developing further the meaning and implications of Humanism as a position, Lamont finds himself forced to confront the problem, posed by statements of the *religious* Humanists, of whether Humanism is to be called a religion. His answer is clearly, No, but the circumstances under which this answer is given are of more than ordinary interest. He begins by attacking 'current redefinitions' of religion; 'As for the word *religion*', he says, 'I think that current redefinitions of it are particularly confusing, since they bring under the heading of religion such very different and in some cases positively irreligious phenomena as nationalism, communism and even atheism' (p. 181). He finds this particularly true of the Humanist Manifesto issued by the religious Humanists where, he claims, 'It is evident the the *Manifesto* makes religion cover practically everything that men do' (p. 182).[6] It was precisely with this problem in mind that the concept of quasi-religions was introduced to describe movements, positions, total outlooks on life which are not to be called religions proper, but which manifest concerns similar to these religions and function in an analogous way in human life. Accordingly, I call Humanism a quasi-religion but not a religion proper. Lamont has a less dialectical approach and seeks to resolve the problem simply by calling a human activity a religion only when it involves an appeal to faith in supernatural elements or states of being. This solution, however, only perpetuates what was described earlier on as the futile see-saw of ascription and denial, but from the other side. If those redefining religion are at fault for making it so broad that it must include Humanism,

Lamont and his followers are likewise guilty in defining religion very narrowly in terms of what is, as far as the analysis goes, a vague notion of the 'supernatural' in order to make sure that Humanism is *not* included. We must overcome this fruitless struggle over the expansion and contraction of 'religion' to suit one purpose or another and return to the experiential situation in which it is quite clear that religion is a pervasive dimension of human experience and is not identical with the world religions. Dewey, no defender of the supernatural, recognised this fact in his attempt to define and defend what he called 'the religious' in experience which stands over against both 'religion' and the 'religions'. Lamont appears to see the point as well when he claims that there is 'an historic function of religion' – finding oneself in consecration to an ideal – which it is the task of any philosophy, presumably including Humanism, to fulfil. It is the existence of the religious concern throughout experience, a concern that is felt not only by the followers of the religions proper, that makes possible the appearance of surrogates aiming to fulfil that concern. In order to stay as close to the descriptive as possible and to avoid the use of pejorative expressions such as 'pseudo-religions', and secular substitutes I employ the term 'quasi-religions' as the best way of pointing up the similarities and analogies involved between certain movements and the religions proper while at the same time staying clear of the charge that one calls any of these movements a 'religion' merely as an act of what one writer has called 'terminological aggression'.

The fact that, according to Humanism, Nature is neutral towards the human race and 'is no more interested in *homo sapiens* than in the tiger, the rat, the extinct Dinosaur' (p. 185), must not lead us to suppose that man is an alien in the world. On the contrary, if this were the case it would be impossible to understand how human beings could have come into being at all. In addition, there is said to be sufficient connection between Nature and human knowledge to make possible the utilisation of Nature for our purposes. Lamont, however, stresses the neutrality of Nature for a more fundamental reason; it allows Humanism to by-pass 'the so-called "problem of evil" with which theologians and philosophers have wrestled throughout the centuries' (p. 186). For the Humanist, this problem does not exist; there are evils only in relation to human life and conduct and it is a mistake to attribute to the universe categories like good and evil which are appropriate for human conduct and whatever is relevant to it. The traditional Christian

attitude toward evil, says Lamont, is itself an evil because it as-
cribes to evil 'a fearful cosmic importance' which has evil effects on
human beings, both psychologically and morally. Concentrating
entirely on the belief that it is the 'mysterious' character of evil, and
especially of pain, which must be dispelled, Lamont tells us that if
'we turn to a scientific analysis of pain in terms of biology and
psychology, there is no mystery at all' (p. 188). Another way of
putting this point is that, in the language of Dewey, there are
legitimate 'retail' questions about particular evils in the world,
their causes and remedies, but that there is no 'wholesale' question
about the existence of evil as such. For both Dewey and Lamont
that is an insoluble question, and, worse, spending time trying to
answer it diverts attention and energy away from trying to do
away with specific evils.

Humanism places supreme confidence in science and the use of
reason in all human affairs, because science has shown its superiority to all other presumed ways of knowing by its self-critical
approach and the appeal to testing. Science, says Lamont, is ethic-
ally neutral and he rightly points out that the use of science for evil
purposes – waging mechanised warfare or attempting genocide – is
a matter of human corruption and is not to be laid at the door of
science itself.

The ethics of Humanism, according to Lamont, is firmly rooted in
an affirmation of life – this life – and is opposed to ascetic other-
worldliness or 'puritanical' morality. It is not an ethics of guilt
stemming from belief in human wickedness, but rather one of
'reasonable self-restraint'. This position is essentially a utilitarian
one in the tradition of Bentham and Mill. 'For Humanism', Lamont
writes, 'no human acts are good or bad in and of themselves' but
are to be judged solely in terms of their good or bad consequences
for the individual and society' (p. 278). Kant's ethics of motives and
a good will is said to be the result of his mind-body dualism which
in turn led to an exaggeration of the role played by motives in
human behaviour. On the other hand, Lamont does not want to go
to the opposite extreme and deny the place of motives altogether,
since that would make it impossible to distinguish, as we do,
between an act of accidental manslaughter and murder with deliberate intent. Motives, nevertheless, are to be appraised in terms
of their consequences, but they retain their importance for Humanism because one of its great aims is 'the transformation and social-
ization of human motives' (p. 288). Such transformation is to come

about through ethical training and the development of social and humanitarian motives that transcend self-interest.

On the political side, Humanism is said to go hand in hand with Democracy. 'The most effective manner of summarizing', Lamont writes, 'the social and economic aims of Humanism is to say that this philosophy supports the widest possible extension of democracy to all relevant aspects of human living' (pp. 310–11). Lamont quotes with approval Reinhold Niebuhr's well-known epigram, 'Man's capacity for justice makes democracy possible; but man's inclination to injustice makes democracy necessary', and he sees one of the tasks of Humanism to clarify the meaning of democracy so that it will be understood in the dual sense of a means or method in government and a goal for human life.

One of the most interesting features of the programme for Humanism set forth by Lamont is the need for artists and writers in a Humanist society 'to work out rituals and ceremonies' that are consistent with the beliefs of Humanism and should 'appeal to the emotions as well as the minds of people, capturing their imagination and giving an outlet to their delight in pomp and pageantry' (p. 306). As it turns out, however, these artists and writers are not so much to be engaged in working out new rituals as they are in recycling in Humanist terms the religious rituals already in existence. Thus Christmas would become a folk-day symbolising the joy of existence, the feeling of human brotherhood and the ideal of democratic sharing. Easter 'can be humanistically utilised' to celebrate the renewal of the vital forces of Nature and the energies of man. There will also be a need for Humanist wedding and funeral services devoid of all supernatural trappings and, in fact, Lamont has written and published *A Humanist Funeral Service*.[7]

Unlike Auguste Comte's religion of Humanity that embraced the formation of churches and a kind of worship of the ideal of Humanity, Lamont's Humanism does not extend this far which is to say that, while man is surely at the centre of this philosophy, there does not appear to be any place for the 'worship' of humanity or indeed for worship of any sort.

Much has happened in the Humanist movement since the publication of Lamont's *Humanism as a Philosophy* in 1949. Of special interest is a collection of essays entitled, *The Humanist Alternative: Some Definitions of Humanism*.[8] These essays are noteworthy in at least three important respects; they focus on the continuing problem of defining and identifying Humanism and in so doing reveal the existence of a plurality of Humanisms; they raise the question of Humanism as a religion and especially the meaning to be given to the expression 'religious Humanism'; finally, they indicate the spread of Humanism to countries throughout the world. I shall consider these three focal points in order.

Kurtz's essay, 'Is Everyone a Humanist?' is aimed at identifying Humanism in such a way that its meaning will not become so attenuated that it cannot be distinguished from other outlooks on life. He begins by applying to Humanism what William James described as the three-stage career of a theory at the hands of its opponents; first, it is attacked as absurd, then it is admitted to be true but obvious, and finally it is seen to be so important that its adversaries claim to have discovered it first. In Kurtz's version, Humanism was a daring idea when first proposed and was ridiculed and attacked; subsequently its critics concede, though reluctantly, that it makes a point, and, finally, it becomes fashionable and a part of received opinion. This situation is what prompts Kurtz to pose the question that is the title of his essay; if everyone is a 'Humanist' what differential meaning can the position have.

Kurtz is thus led to attempt to recover essential Humanism and to rescue it from those who would appropriate it for themselves. He cites certain statements by Pope Paul VI and other Catholic authorities which declare that 'Christianity is a Humanism . . . based on God' and this he finds both objectionable and ironic since Humanism rejects the supernatural and the Catholic Church has often suppressed free thought. The early Marx, he notes, declared himself a Humanist, but the Communism he inspired presents a contradictory picture. Orthodox Communists claim that 'Communism is the only real Humanism', but those who oppose that orthodoxy with the images of Lenin and Stalin before them also appeal to Humanism as their standard. There are, moreover, Kurtz says, liberal democrats who profess to be Humanists as well as Jews, Zen Buddhists and Protestants so that he finds the situation quite bewildering. 'The term "Humanism" ', he writes,

is now an 'in' word. But Humanism is so charged with levels of emotion and rhetoric that its meaning is often vague and ambiguous. It is in danger of being inundated and destroyed by those who do not really believe in it. (Kurtz, p. 176)

To remedy the situation, Kurtz proposes to make clear the descript-element in the meaning of Humanism which will enable us to determine who is a Humanist and who is not, for, as he says, 'It would be a cardinal mistake to allow the meaning of Humanism to be polluted by its detractors' (Kurtz, p. 177). The task, then, is first to indicate what Humanism is *not* or is not to be identified with and to follow up with a statement of what it is. Humanism, above all, excludes belief in God or a Creator, but with the proviso that 'religious Humanism' is not to be excluded as long as it is a 'naturalistic non-theism'. Humanism is not of itself a political programme or a political ideology; it is not an emotional commitment to 'a vague humanitarianism' nor is it to be equated with liberalism because that would, for example, rule out an avowed Humanist like Santayana who was conservative in his political views.

On the positive side – although these elements also involve negations – Humanism is based on a scientific view of man and nature and is opposed to 'mythological illusions' – religious or ideological – about man's place in the universe. Humanism, though radically critical of all supernatural theories, is not committed to any particular metaphysical position and hence it can incorporate materialism, evolutionary naturalism and organicism. For Kurtz, it is of the utmost importance that Humanism be seen primarily as a *moral* viewpoint emphasising the values of self-preservation, creative self-realisation and happiness. To develop autonomous, free agents is the goal, but this is not to be taken to mean an individualism that turns its back on the basically social nature of all human life.

An important feature of Kurtz's account of Humanism is the self-critical spirit he seeks to include and warns against falling prey to 'liberal Humanist clichés or myths'. He stresses the importance of experience as a guide and makes some realistic observations about the ambiguities that surround all movements and programmes in society. Humanists, he says, supported the growth of science and technology but they need to be aware of the dehumanisation that advanced technology brings with it, together with threats to the ecological system. Likewise, Humanists have hailed Democracy as the hope of mankind, but according to Kurtz, there must not be too much participatory democracy in educational institutions because it can lead to 'the vulgarization of learning and the destruction of standards of excellence' (Kurtz, p. 181). Humanists have supported sexual liberation and a tolerant attitude towards sexuality, but an uncritical approach to the sexual revolution can lead to the dehumanising of sex, pornography and the exploitation of people as sex objects. A similar ambiguity is said to be present in the sympathy Humanists have shown to socialism, but oppression, the denial of human rights – freedom of speech and artistic creation – and authoritarianism have all made their appearance in socialist regimes.

Kurtz also warns Humanists against worshipping 'the myth of Progress' and believing in 'an inevitable march of human history' (Kurtz, p. 182).[9] In a final attempt to say what Humanism essentially is, Kurtz singles out the ideal of free thought and opposition to all forms of tyranny over the mind of man. In addition to their moral ideals all Humanists share a commitment to the use of critical intelligence and the use of tolerance, dialogue and negotiations in all attempts to resolve human problems. In the end, however, a negative note creeps in when this Humanism is said to identified by a rejection of theistic religion and totalitarian ideology.

H. J. Blackham in his essay, 'A Definition of Humanism', adds an interesting dimension to the discussion with his distinction between a concept of human nature and a concept of man. The former would be 'a synthesis of relevant knowledge on which general agreement could be expected' (Kurtz, p. 35), whereas concepts of man 'go beyond information and are presumably purely speculative in character'. What he has in mind is the basic idea that man is sick and not his true self as depicted by Christianity through 'fallen' man, by Marxism through 'alienation' and by existentialism through the 'inauthentic'. In each case, he says, 'there is a justifying total view and a dependent strategy for living' so that man is supposed to become his true self by obedience to the divine will, by identifying with the historical process or by accepting responsibility for a continuous exercise of freedom. Whether Blackham is aware of it or not, he is referring here to what was previously described as a structure in the religions proper that begins with a diagnosis of the human predicament and seeks for a way of deliverance. Humanism, however, does not stress the difference between what man is and what he ought to be, nor does it view man in terms of some universal end that is already determined. Blackham is quite explicit in identifying his understanding of Humanism; human responsibility is the key concept; 'there is', he writes,

no entelechy, no built-in pattern of perfection. Man is his own rule and his own end. (Kurtz, p. 36)

This characterisation of Humanism makes more explicit its final and total emphasis on man as the centre of reality than definitions in terms of free inquiry or the rejection of the supernatural.

Sidney Hook in 'The Snare of Definitions' further points up the difficulties encountered in the effort to define Humanism. We are, he says, to avoid the extreme of defining it too narrowly less we exclude those who have a moral kinship with Humanism but also have metaphysical or even theological 'overbeliefs'[10] that Humanists find uncongenial. We are also, however, to avoid the pitfall of defining too broadly for in that case no one is excluded – 'If the Holy Grail is everywhere there is no point in its quest' (Kurtz, p. 32). It appears that Hook is more concerned with the latter error and he points out that since no one denies the value of man, there is no need to make the saying attributed to Protagoras, 'Man is the measure of all things' a necessary element in the definition of Humanism because it would exclude such Humanists as Socrates and Bertrand Russell who rejected the Protagorean assertion.

Horace Friess in his essay, 'Humanist Responsibilities' clearly recognises a plurality of Humanisms in what he calls the 'qualifications' of scientific, ethical and religious Humanism. Scientific Humanism emphasises the reliable knowledge we need as a resource for effective operations and for understanding the continuity of man and nature. Ethical Humanism focuses on integrity and justice in the treatment of persons and groups, and embraces an ethic of compassion in a world of suffering. Religious Humanism is primarily a dedication to Humanist values and the nurturing of a faith in them. It also moves in the direction of a 'cosmic range of feeling, appreciation and apprehension' (Kurtz, p. 41). Friess advocates cooperation between these three types lest 'they thwart one another by illusory estimates of their own competences' (ibid.).

J. P. Van Praag addresses his question, 'What is Humanism?' by distinguishing between an unambiguous definition and a clarifying description; the former are possible only in science and in theoretical frameworks, while the latter are more appropriate for indicating the existential value and moral conviction represented by Humanism.[11] Van Praag's goals are somewhat more ambitious than those of other contributors in that he wants his description to be *clear* enough to identify Humanism as distinct from other positions, but *broad* enough to include 'all varieties of Humanism, such aesthetical, scientific, religious and social varieties of the basic idea' (Kurtz, p. 43). Thus, like Friess, Van Praag recognises several types of Humanism based on different emphases, but unified, nevertheless, by certain beliefs shared by all. We may, he says, approach the desired description by attending to what Humanism starts from, a phenomenological account, or by focusing on what it stands for, a statement of aims. He proposes ten postulates meant to describe what Humanism starts from. We may list these postulates and indicate briefly what each contributes to the total picture.

1. Equality. Men are everywhere of a similar biological and mental structure and in view of this fact, differences between human beings become irrelevant. Equality is the basis for all to have a common world.
2. Secularity. Men spring from a world of which they are a natural part; they are a unity of body and consciousness and intentionally shape the world.
3. Freedom. Men shape their lives by deciding in freedom; through self-determination life is given meaning.
4. Fraternity. Men are designated for community and are shaped by it; community provides for the meaning of life and a standard of moral judgement.
5. Evaluation. Men are evaluating beings by applying reason.
6. Experience. The world is experienced by identification and observation; identification is synthetical and provides religious experience; observation is analytical and provides knowledge.
7. Existence. Men and world exist coherently together and are interdependent; the world is a human world and men are secular beings.
8. Completeness The world is complete, but not perfect; it is not dependent on a creator.
9. Evolution. The world is dynamic in an evolution that develops in lawful coherence, enabling men to live with reality and act upon it.
10. Contingency. The world by itself does not reveal meaning. Man can contribute meaning to his existence by his interpretation of reality. (Kurtz, p. 44)

This outline, says Van Praag, 'by no means represents the variety of Humanist conceptions', but sets forth the common basis of Humanist thinking and action (ibid.). He proposes to express the common aims of the 'various types of Humanism' as follows:

Humanism is a moral conviction characterized by the attempt to understand life and the world and to act in it by appealing exclusively to human faculties; and it is directed towards everyone's self-determination in a common humanity. It naturally considers all fixed positions as subject to discussion. However, it reminds us of certain ideas that under varying circumstances must be converted into concrete purposes. Some of these basic conceptions can serve not so much to explain Humanism as to clarify what it aims at. (Kurtz, p. 45)

It will be helpful to call attention to some elements in the list of postulates and the above statement which are most relevant for our discussion of the extent to which a plurality of Humanisms is recognised and, ultimately, to the discussion of Humanism as a quasi-religion. To begin with, Van Praag is concerned to avoid reducing Humanism to but one of its aspects or emphases, at the same time he wants to show its difference from other positions. Accordingly, he makes room within experience for religious experience through what is called identification and thus leaves the door open for religious Humanism. In speaking of 'secularity' and of people as 'secular beings', he is using the term more in the sense of man being in the world and a natural part of it, than in the sense of an opposition to religion, or what is called by most Humanists, the supernatural, although that note is sounded in the idea that the world is complete and independent of a creator. Finally, there is the belief, not unlike Lamont's claim that Nature is neutral as regards man and his judgements of right and wrong, good and evil, that the world reveals no meaning but what man can contribute to his life through the interpretation of reality.

What may we conclude from the foregoing efforts to characterise Humanism as an identifiable outlook on life? First, it seems clear that a number of writers are concerned to define Humanism in a way sufficiently clear that it becomes a position distinguishable from others and to avoid the consequence that 'everyone is a Humanist'. On the other hand, as we have seen, there is also expressed the concern not to exclude from the Humanist camp forms of Humanism that have actually established themselves such as religious Humanism and Ethical Culture Societies. Second, it is equally clear that there exist varieties of Humanism based on differences of emphasis, whether the ethical, the scientific, the social, the naturalistic or the religious, and that there is tension among them with respect to what is 'true' Humanism. Thirdly, the feature most appealed to in the effort to make sure that Humanism is not confused with any other outlook is secularity, in its several senses, this-worldliness, the independence of the world from a creator and the centrality of man as his own end and ruler. In this respect, Humanism gains its principal identity as standing over against what it takes to be characteristic of what I have been calling the religions proper.

We may now turn to the second topic previously cited – the question whether Humanism is to be called a 'religion,' or, if not that, whether it can be said to have a 'religious' character. The picture is rather complicated in virtue of the fact that reference is made to 'religious Humanism', to 'Humanistic Theism' and to Humanism being a 'certain religious temper'. It is to be noted, moreover, that these are designations made by Humanists about their own position; they are not ascriptions made by those outside the fold. Herbert W. Schneider in his essay, 'Religious Humanism' insists on a distinction between Humanism as a religion, and religion interpreted as a form of human expression, and says that there is confusion since the term 'religious Humanism' has been used to cover both. He sees Humanist religion as 'an effort to free religious faith and devotion from the dogmas of theistic theologies and supernaturalist psychologies' (Kurtz, p. 65) on the part of those who have been alienated from religious institutions because of their opposition to these doctrines. Consequently, says Schneider, they see religion in essentially individualistic terms and hesitate to establish a sect or religious organisation. Instead, they formulate a creed and 'avoid religious rites', remaining a militant minority dedicated to the defiance of theistic beliefs while continuing to insist that their faith is religious. Humanist interpretations of religion, on the other hand, are seen as reform movements within particular religions aimed at the elimination of superstitious beliefs and find their guide in what William James called a 'science of religions' aimed at determining the generic structure of religion for purposes of comparison. 'Assuming that a religion is neither true nor false as a whole', Schneider writes, 'Humanists attempt to make a critical evaluation of religions and to determine when and how religions are good or evil' (Kurtz, p. 66). Schneider, as is obvious, is far less inclined than many Humanists to characterise Humanism as totally opposed to religion, but tries to make room for a religious Humanism as well as to recognise the need for a Humanist critique of certain features in the religious traditions.

Gardner Williams, however, in his essay 'Humanistic Theism' goes much further and appeals to a distinction between two ideas both present in the idea of God. One is the 'basic physical cosmic *substance;*' the other is 'the ideal of the highest good, the *summum bonum*, the goal of man's ultimate rational devotion' (Kurtz, p. 68). After noting Santayana's claim that there is a 'grand contradiction' in identifying the two, Williams proposes a resolution of the difficulty. 'In order to avoid this muddled ideology', Williams writes, 'I suggest that we call the basic physical substance of the cosmos the *supreme being*, and save the word God for the ideal of Man's highest good' (Kurtz, p. 68). The supreme being is said to be omnipotent, participating in and producing all actual events, and does everything that is done, both good and evil. It has produced 'mostly unintentionally' life, consciousness, purpose and reason, together with all the grandeur of experience. It also, however, has caused despair, anguish, suffering and death and thus, in being evil, is not to be worshipped; to do so would be idolatrous.

God, however, is another matter. Using Santayana's ideas about essences and potentiality, existing and subsisting, Williams argues that God is a real fact since He is something about which one can tell the truth. This truth is that God as the highest good ought to exist because 'people would be so much happier if He were actualized in their lives' (ibid.). And this truth, he continues, can be a truth only if God is a fact. God, then, is to be understood as a 'real, factual, nonexistent (i.e. subsistent) potential'. Man's whole duty is to make the actual conform as far as possible to the ideal of the supreme good. 'Man's first duty is to God' and this is Humanistic Theism. It is important to take note of the order of the terms; this position is not a theistic humanism, but rather a reinterpretation of God in accordance with Humanist ideals so as to provide a basis for the sort of Humanism upheld by the Fellowship of Religious Humanists.

Further light is thrown on the relation between Humanism and religion by Bernard Phillips in his essay, 'Zen and Humanism', where he shows some similarities between the two, but also points to a basic ambiguity in Humanism concerning what constitutes being human. For our purposes it will not be necessary to raise questions about Phillips's interpretation of Zen, since what is of the main importance is his commentary on Humanism from that vantage point. According to him, Zen is three things; first, a particular sect of Buddhism with its own history and institutionalised forms;

second, it is the heart of Buddhism and, being without scriptures, points to the ultimate source of Buddhism which is the enlighten- ment experience of the Buddha; third, Zen aims to transcend the particularities of Buddhism so that it can be called religion itself 'in its most universal intention' (Kurtz, p. 159). Zen, in short, is the life of authentic being, 'wherein the self has overcome its alienation from itself and all other things' (ibid.), and when Zen is realised it transcends even itself and 'bows out of being' (ibid.).

From this perspective, Phillips puts some questions to the Hu- manists, the first of which is what is meant by 'human'. All meta- physical thought, he says, is directed to clarifying the mutual status of nature, man and God so that 'the Humanist has finally to declare his own understanding of the matter' (ibid.). Phillips sees Human- ism as battling on two fronts; it has struggled to preserve the independence of the human against the divine, but it has also to guard the human against the brutishness and darkness of nature which, as he sees it, means defending the importance of the Humanities against the encroachments of the natural sciences. The question is, shall man direct himself primarily to 'to *natur*, to *kultur* or to *geist*?' (Kurtz, p. 160). It is important, he continues, to under- stand man's ultimate needs and whether they are to be met through increasing mastery over nature; 'is there in the human heart', he asks, 'an irrepressible longing for an overcoming of the alienation from its own ground?' (ibid.). Phillips is clearly pressing Human- ists to respond to this question and in so doing to identify their fundamental orientation. Humanism and Zen, he says, are both abstractions and when viewed as philosophical positions, as 'isms', they have no power to nourish life. Zen, however, knows itself to be an abstraction and hence has no desire to perpetuate itself as a system and, in fact, being a 'Zen Buddhist' is only a temporary designation for someone who is en route 'towards the goal of discovering his nameless self' (ibid.).

'Is [Humanism]', he asks, 'similarly oriented towards its own eventual dissolution', or is it rather a position to be adhered to for the sake of an identity? (Kurtz, p. 161). But what is the basis of an identity? Since Zen holds that the true identity of man is 'not merely a natural datum', but has to be created and discovered, any nominal or conventional identity gained through adopting a posi- tion can be nothing more than a pose or posture, a shield against the threat of nothingness. According to Zen, however, there can be a real identity for man, but it cannot reside in a position. While Zen is said to be beyond Humanism or any other 'ism', Phillips takes note of the humanist component in Buddhism in that it accords central importance to man and bids him to save himself by his own efforts. But in the end, he says, 'Buddhism in general and Zen in particular cannot be equated with Humanism' because it is religion and possesses 'what Humanism lacks, namely cosmic rootage' (Kurtz, p. 164). The Enlightenment of which Zen speaks is something more than psychological and moral development; 'it is an overcoming of the dualism of finite and infinite, of the alienation of the finite from its ground, which is to say it has a spiritual dimension as well as a humanistic and moral one' (Kurtz, p. 164). What Phillips is driving at is twofold; on the one hand, he wants to show that there is a religious dimension involved in the meaning of 'what is truly human' and that many forms of Humanism leave this out of account, and, on the other, he is claiming that the Humanism characteristic of both Confucius and Socrates is one that has to be *lived* in order to become known, which is the reason, according to Phillips, why neither answered their pupils' inquiries in terms of an abstract definition of manhood. The identity Zen seeks is expressed in the phrase 'man with no title' which means that man is not to be conceptualised, defined or confined. 'The paradox', Phillips writes,

> is that where identity can be identified, it is not true identity but only nominal or conventional identity. The man of real identity cannot be identified. He is real, not a label . . . He *is* his identity. (Kurtz, p. 165)

The conclusion Phillips draws is that Humanism as a position cannot identify true manhood, or rather that if it does identify man through an 'ism' it misses the truth about human nature. We shall return to this essay later on in the comparison between Humanism and the religions proper.

The third topic mentioned above focused by the essays we have been considering – the spread of various types of Humanism throughout the world – is more historical than philosophical in nature, but it represents an important part of the total picture. The authors are writers, educators, psychologists, philosophers and political scientists and, in addition to those from America and Britain, there are contributors from the Soviet Union, India, France and Holland. Among the organisations represented are The New York Society for Ethical Culture, The British Humanist Association,

The Atheist Centre in Vijayawada, India, l'Institute de l'Homme in Paris, the American Humanist Association, the American Ethical Union, the Secular Society of Great Britain, the Fellowship of Religious Humanists and the International Humanist and Ethical Union. There is considerable variety in the sort of activities in which these groups are engaged. The Societies for Ethical Culture hold weekly meetings with lectures and addresses delivered by a leader or an invited speaker. Other groups sponsor conferences and symposia about Humanist principles and moral, social and political issues and many of their members serve as editors and contributors to such journals as *The Humanist* and more recently *Free Inquiry*.

Since the publication of *The Humanist Alternative* in 1973, a number of further developments have taken place in the Humanist movement and to these we now turn. First, there was the formation of the Council for Democratic and Secular Humanism and the founding in 1980 of *Free Inquiry*, a quarterly journal which provides a forum for the expression of Humanist beliefs both about the position itself and the application of its principles and values to problems ranging from nuclear war to child abuse. The council also sponsors a number of projects aimed at carrying out Humanist goals. One such project was the establishing of The Academy of Humanism in order to 'recognize distinguished humanists' ideals and beliefs'. Those thus honoured, 'Humanist Laureates', as they are called, are identified primarily as 'nontheists' who are devoted to the ideals of Humanism as set forth in 'A Statement of Principles and Values' constituting what is called 'The Affirmation of Humanism'. This document lists 21 particular beliefs and goals which include belief in reason and science, rejection of the supernatural and opposition to 'theologies of despair and ideologies of violence'. Among those who have been honoured by the Academy are Sir A. J. Ayer, Sir Isaiah Berlin, Betty Friedan, Stephen J. Gould, Adolf Grünbaum, W. V. Quine, Carl Sagan, Brand Blanshard and Ernest Nagel.

In addition to the Academy, the Council has also formed a Committee for the Scientific Exploration of Religion aimed at examining the 'claims of Eastern and Western religions and of well established and newer sects and denominations in the light of scientific inquiry'. This Committee has, in turn, formed two subcommittees; one is called the Biblical Criticism Research Project and the other a Faith-Healing Investigation Project. It becomes clear, and I shall illustrate the point by noting the topics discussed in a typical issue of *Free Inquiry* plus a selection of topics from other issues, that much of the effort expended in these projects is directed against any attempt to classify Humanism as a religion, and, more importantly, to attack Fundamentalist religious beliefs and practices, especially creationism versus science and faith-healing versus medical attention. The irony here is extreme; the religious intelligence of non-Fundamentalist Christianity as represented by Tillich, Barth, the Niebuhrs and the liberal Catholic Rahner, to name but a few, is as much opposed as the Humanists are to these same beliefs and practices. Humanists tend to overlook this fact because of their simplistic and uncritical use of the term 'supernatural' – surely as elusive a term as 'Humanism' – to lump together all religion in an indiscriminate way. Prophets of reason and science must be expected to do better.

In the issue of *Free Inquiry* for Spring, 1989, the basic theme is 'Living Without Religion; The Ethics of Humanism' and one of the main aims is to show that there can be morality without religion and that Humanism can provide the roots needed for morality. A noteworthy development is found in Paul Kurtz's attempt to offer a more refined description (not a new definition) of secular Humanism as a 'Eupraxophy' – a term made up from the Greek *eu* (good, well), *praxis* (activity or conduct) and *sophia* (knowledge, wisdom). Kurtz introduced the term some years earlier in an article with a revealing title, 'Eupraxophy: Breaking with the Old Humanism',[12] and he develops its meaning further in the issue under discussion. 'As a Eupraxophy', he writes, 'humanism has four main characteristics':

1. It is a method of inquiry that uses reason and evidence to test claims to truth and that advocates the use of critical intelligence in dealing with human problems.
2. Its cosmic outlook is based upon the findings of science, rather than on mere metaphysical speculation.
3. Its ethical values and principles are concerned with enhancing the good life here on earth.
4. It has social polity, advocating democracy and human freedom.

In a summary comment Kurtz claims that 'None of these characteristics are "religious" per se'. The main reason for this new description of Humanism is to separate it as completely as possible from the 'religious'. Such a separation, he argues, is necessary 'because virtually all of the official humanist organizations in the

United States consider themselves to be religious'. Kurtz will have none of that; 'Let us be forthright:' he says, 'Secular humanism is a form of atheism or agnosticism'. Here the identification of this humanism as the rejection of religion in any sense becomes most explicit. Kurtz's humanism may have many positive principles and goals, but the recurrent theme in this new description is the negative distancing of humanism from religion, even if the term 'Eupraxophy' does not express the fact. This negativity, moreover, is clearly reflected in the titles of other articles in this issue: 'The Morality of Unbelief', 'Scientific Knowledge, Moral Knowledge: Is There Any Need for Faith?', 'The Study of the Gospels as Literary Fiction'. A similar attitude is expressed in the articles to be found in a large number of the issues of *Free Inquiry* starting with the first. Here is a sampling: 'Morality Without Religion', 'Resurrection Fictions', 'Biblical Criticism and Its Discontents', 'The Winter Solstice and the Origin of Christmas', 'The "Escape-Goat" of Christianity', 'The Relativity of Biblical Ethics', and many more in a similar vein.

All of this evidence tends to show the strongly negative tendency that pervades, if not Humanism in general, at least this particular version of it. The chief targets of attack are Fundamentalism, the belief in faith-healing and the practices of charismatic sects. But once again there is present the same irony we saw before: 'main line Protestantism' – for want of a better name – has been no less vigorous in its rejection of these distortions of religion than Humanism has shown itself to be. This fact, however, is buried under a bushel of indiscriminate thinking about religion and a simplistic identification of all religion with something called the 'supernatural' a sort of catch-all term used on every occasion but rarely with any other than a negative meaning derived from the contrast with the term 'nature' or the domain that is presumed to be the special province of Humanists.[13]

The foregoing description and exposition of Humanism, albeit brief in the face of the protean character of this movement, has been aimed at allowing typical representatives of this position to speak for themselves, and with a few exceptions I have refrained from critical commentary because my aim is to show how we can understand Humanism as a quasi-religion. For that purpose it is necessary to have the position presented in as accurate a way as possible, especially in order to avoid the quite futile argument, sometimes carried on among Humanists themselves, as to whether it is 'religion' or 'religious'. I hope to show further how the concept of a quasi-religion can help to get beyond that dispute and at the same time illuminate how Humanism stands in comparison with what I have been calling the religions proper.

We need to bear in mind that to speak of all the forms of Humanism together is at the least very difficult and at the most impossible. For, among other things, there is the problem of how to characterise the Humanism that calls itself religious. I suggest that we let that form of Humanism stand for itself and if its adherents regard it as religion, then there is no need to interpret it as a quasi-religion. Hence the comparisons that follow will be oriented in the direction of naturalistic and secular Humanism where the anti-religious note is most often sounded and where the aim is to replace religion which is one of the principal reasons why I regard it as a quasi-religion.

There are, at the outset, two most obvious contrasts between Humanism and the religions proper; the first is the absence of a supremely worshipful reality. Even though humanity is said to stand at the centre, and Nature is the term through which all reality is identified, neither for Humanism is the subject of the worshipful attitude characteristic of the world religions, East and West. This state of affairs may be due less to the absence of belief in a worshipful reality in Humanism, than to its negative view of worship itself. If man is his own end and rule and there is reluctance to talk about 'worshipping' man, whom or what, we may ask, would there be to worship? However, even if there is no counterpart for worship in the widely illustrated religious sense – involving awe, devotion, gratitude – Humanism nevertheless, has its *ultimate allegiances*. These take the form of reason and science, free inquiry, democracy, a naturalistic outlook, opposition to the supernatural, to name but a few, all of which, if we take seriously what Humanists say, demand from them an *unconditional loyalty*.

The second clear contrast between Humanism and the religions proper is that there is in Humanism nothing that corresponds very closely to what was previously described as a diagnosis of a human predicament, or the acknowledgement of some fundamental flaw, some source of disorientation or alienation in human beings as they naturally are. The reason for this lack is to be found in Humanism's naturalistic philosophical outlook and its one-dimensional view. The issue was focused earlier on in connection with H.J. Blackham's essay (see p. 29) in which he distinguishes between a concept of human nature and a concept of man. The former, on this view, is based on relevant knowledge about which all are supposed to agree, whereas a concept of man expresses ideas that 'go beyond information'.

But more precisely what is this relevant knowledge? The human species has been the subject of study by many sciences and unless we are to suppose that the results are somehow all brought together in anthropology, which is but one discipline among others, it is by no means clear what conception of human nature emerges about which there is general agreement. What it means to be human cannot simply be read off, as it were, from knowledge about what human beings have in the past experienced, created, destroyed, believed in, eaten, discovered about themselves and the world, hoped for, etc. and for two reasons; first, it is in fact not possible to avoid a basic selective emphasis in determining what being human means, for example, that the human mind is the key, or the capacity to make tools, or the exercise of freedom, or the capacity to laugh, etc. We can recite all the facts that have been recorded by the sciences studying man, but without such an emphasis or a principle of organisation no conception of human nature will emerge. Second, it is not to be supposed that the 'naturalistic' picture of being human which is dominant in most forms of Humanism represents the voice of 'science' while all other pictures are merely 'metaphysical'. Here we must distinguish between knowledge about man, howsoever relevant, and the voice of the naturalistic philosopher which claims to be speaking in terms of science and nothing but science. In short, everyone, including Humanists, is engaged in presenting what Blackham calls a 'conception of man' which is to say a philosophical picture of the *same logical type* as the pictures offered by Plato, Aristotle, Kant, Marx or Dewey. Humanism tends to obscure this fact in claiming that its picture is simply what science tells us without extrapolation.

This sort of contention is absolutely essential to Humanism and it is often presented as if it were clear as day and incontestable. Science, presumably, gives us knowledge of human nature or of a 'natural' animal who lives in an environing world wherein social, political, economic and cultural institutions are developed in an ongoing course of history. This picture expresses what human nature 'really is' without recourse to the supposedly metaphysical or religious fictions that are responsible for producing extra-scientific conceptions of 'man' in which there is a fundamental contrast between a 'fallen', 'alienated', 'desire-bound', or 'inauthentic' type of existence and an ideal life in which these obstacles are overcome.

The same point is raised by Bernard Phillips (see p. 35) when he challenges Humanists to clarify what is meant by being human. And, of course, what he is driving at is the need to approach the question by attending to the interdependence of the three members of what was called 'the Great Chain of Being', Nature, God and man. The meaning of each member is dependent upon the distinctions and contrasts among them, but Humanism tries to collapse this trinity into something called Nature which is supposed to stand for all these is, or, more precisely, whatever is subject to scientific inquiry. But how are we to determine the meaning of a term like Nature or Man which found their initial meaning through contrast with something else, when there is no longer any contrast? The only solution to this problem is to set Nature off against the Supernatural – another protean term – and then include man within Nature while declaring that Nature is all there is.

Although there is in Humanism no diagnosis of the human situation in the explicitly religious sense where the nature of supremely worshipful Being sets the standard for judgement, Humanism has, nevertheless, a diagnosis of another sort. We may call it immanent or piecemeal appraisal which in effect makes clear what Humanism believes is wrong with the state of things in this world. This diagnosis is possible in the first instance because of an appeal to the Humanist principles and values of which we have taken note. There is a vision, this-worldly to be sure, of an ideal human fulfilment – a person of autonomy, freedom, creativity, applying reason and science to human problems, enjoying the beauties of nature and culture, free of superstition (and, for some, of religion as well), striving for democracy throughout the world, an opponent of tyranny and violence, a lover of peace and concord. It is in the name of these normative standards which, as the *Affirmation* puts it, 'we discover together', that Humanism condemns all that it abhors in the human situation from the denigration of reason and the seeking of salvation outside nature to counsels of despair and pessimism which stress guilt or sin instead of joy. The list requires no great effort of the imagination – ignorance, prejudice, superstition, injustice, violence, tyranny and, for some Humanists at least, the very existence of so-called supernatural religion. Recall, for example, that Lamont describes the biblical conception of the problem of evil as depicted in the situation of Job as itself an evil. Hence it is difficult to avoid the conclusion that even for Humanism there is much in human life from which we need to be 'delivered', or which needs to be overcome if the best life possible in this world is to be achieved. If, therefore, there exists what man needs to be delivered from and Humanism insists on optimism as the only appropriate attitude, there must be a quest for a 'deliverer' in some form or other, even if in this case the quest is a short one since it is found ready to hand in the resources of reason, science, free inquiry and a belief in the *control* of nature and of man himself, all of which is deemed sufficient for overcoming human ills. It is, however, not to be supposed that the values Humanists espouse are derivative in any straightforward sense from the sciences. The point needs to be raised because of the number of occasions upon which Dewey – who might be called the adopted patron saint of Humanism – called attention to the erosion in this century of the authority once exercised by moral and religious principles and ideals and pro- posed that the findings of the social sciences should make up the deficiency. Lamont, it will be recalled, did not have this problem since he appropriates for Humanism the insights of philosophers, poets, artists, writers and even beliefs derived from Confucius, Buddha and Jesus, and thus includes within Humanism many values that are far older than modern science.

The point to be emphasised is the large dependence by Human- ists on the power of both science and technology to serve as the deliverer of mankind from the evils that abound. Belief in the efficacy of the control of nature within reasonable limits and self- control in human beings has often been bolstered by another of Dewey's ideas summed up in what used to be called the 'cultural lag'. Writing in the earlier decades of this century, Dewey claimed that the social sciences of the time were in much the same state as the natural sciences were before they discovered the method of experimental control and thus left the pseudo-sciences behind. Dewey believed that when the social sciences 'catch up' and overcome their 'lag' behind the natural sciences, they will find themselves in a similar position to exercise control of conditions and situations in society and human affairs. That this has not happened says a great deal about both the human species and the social sciences.

We may now summarise the reasons for calling Humanism, as it has been presented in the writings of a number of representative Humanists, a quasi-religion. The first, and most obvious reason, is that the majority of its adherents see it as superseding traditional religion or as a way of living without religion. Put more positively, the aim is to fulfil in a this-worldly and naturalistic vein what

Lamont called the function in human experience of traditional religion. Humanism has a central focus in man and in the fullest realisation of the best that human beings are capable of becoming. This focus, together with Humanist beliefs and values, marks out a centre of loyalty and devotion which serves as a way of unifying the self with an order of mutually cooperating persons. There is, moreover, in Humanism a counterpart for the diagnosis/deliverance pattern which, as we have seen, manifests itself as the generic structure of the religions proper. While there is an unwillingness to speak of *the* human predicament in wholistic terms such as we find in Biblical religion, Hinduism and Buddhism, there is, nevertheless, a Humanist diagnosis of the evils surrounding human life in the world which is based on Humanist beliefs about what the best life should be. In this sense Humanism speaks idealistically in its criticism of those beliefs and practices it finds objectionable, but it adopts the stance of the positivists when it comes to doing away not only with supernatural religion but with all non-naturalistic metaphysics. Thus there is an acknowledgement on the part of Humanists that, in the words of James, there is something 'wrong' about us as we naturally stand, except that what evils or ills are recognised are plural in character and do not point to any fundamental flaw in human beings as such. In this respect Humanist diagnosis stands in sharp contrast to what we find in the religions proper. There the flaw in human nature is expressed in specific terms whether in a self-centred rebellion against God and the worshipping of idols as in Biblical religion, in the unregulated desire that is focused on transient things as in Buddhism, or in the ignorance of the truth that *Atman* and *Brahman* are one as in the Vedanta. These diagnoses point to a flaw which is regarded as intractable in the sense that the being who has it is unable to overcome it merely through an act of will and apart from the resources to be found in a divine love, a divine law, the Noble Eightfold Path that sets limits to the boundlessness of natural desire, or the metaphysical insight into the truth about Brahman.

Whatever shortcomings there are in human nature that Humanism recognises are regarded, at least in principle, as tractable in the sense that man has the resources within himself and within this world to overcome them. Man, in short, is his own deliverer, but, to be sure, with the aid of the resources available to him – reason, science, technology, ethical culture, the arts and the structures of society, all guided by Humanist aims and ideals.

3

Marxism as a Quasi-Religion

It might seem that the events of the past few years during which the world has witnessed the dismantling of the Soviet Union – with the possible exception of China, the largest scale attempt ever to realise the aims of Marxism – would render irrelevant, obsolete or both any analysis of Communism as a substitute for religion. On the contrary, these events make such an analysis more pertinent than ever, since we are now in a position to compare the factors that led to the break-up of the Soviet Union with the assessment made of that system by a number of well-known intellectuals who, as we shall see, were sincerely attracted to the Communist cause in the 1930s, but who came ultimately to reject it as a faith that failed.[1] There are close parallels between the reasons offered by these converts to Communism for leaving the Party or repudiating the cause, and the evils in the system itself which were the cause of its downfall. Later on, after we have considered the experiences of Arthur Koestler, Ignazio Silone and others, we shall be in a better position to understand the comparison. In anticipation, however, we may cite three factors that determined these individuals, in the figure of Louis Fischer, 'to leave the train', and that led, through the efforts of Gorbachev and others, to the splintering of the Party and the call for democracy of a sort yet to be worked out.

First and foremost was the tyranny exercised by the Party coupled with the corruption of the bureaucracy and the cynicism that pervaded the political tactics of deceit and betrayal enforced by the KGB. Next was the mentality of 'the end justifies the means, any means' and the supposition that it is allowable to turn men into machines in the 'meantime', since at the final triumph of the revolution, everyone will become human beings again. Third, was the need for massive propaganda of the sort represented by *Pravda* in order to disguise from the rest of the world, not to mention from the Russian peoples themselves, the awesome contradiction

between the avowed ideals of Communism and the actual conditions of life in the Soviet Union.

The term 'Marxism' covers many things and hence it is necessary
at the outset to sharpen our focus especially in view of the fact that
not every aspect of this large topic will be relevant for our purposes. Quite obviously, the primary content of Marxism has to be
the fundamental concepts, principles and ideals for human beings
and society set forth in Marx's many writings, both philosophical
and economic.[2] In addition to this 'canon', we must include within
Marxism a vast body of commentary on Marx's works together
with a no less vast body of 'revisions' of his thought stretching from
Trotsky and Lenin to Mao Zedong. Marxism must also be understood as signifying political regimes and forms of communism
which purport to represent the realisation of Marx's vision of a
non-exploitative society in which the disinherited would receive
fair treatment and enjoy the fruits of their labour.

In considering Marxism as a quasi-religion it will be necessary to
concentrate chiefly on Marx's basic ideas for, despite the tendency
of many Marxists to disparage theory or even to claim that there
is in Marxism no 'surplus' theory or speculation, i.e., no theory that
is not set to work as a revolutionary instrument, the fact remains
that the great appeal of Marxism has always been its dramatic
vision of a new human being in a new society to be brought about
by revolutionary activity with the help of the dialectic of history.
One may even say that it is Marx's initial vision that has continued
to provide the dynamic of Marxism and to serve as the basis of
its wide appeal. Without this vision as its main source of attraction, it is not likely that vast numbers of people would have
embraced Marxism solely on the basis of seeing what actually
happened in Communist regimes where it was supposedly put into
practice!

The discussion will be divided into two parts; the first will set
forth Marx's main ideas and indicate, in the terms laid out thus far,
the ingredients in Marxism which enable it to function as a quasi-
religion. The second part will offer some further insight into not
only what makes it possible for Marxism to function in this way,
but also into some illustrations from the experience of several noted
individuals for whom Marxism had actually become a substitute
religion, even if in the end it proved inadequate.

It has often been said, and rightly, that Marx's thought cannot be
understood without taking into account those ideas contained in

Hegel's philosophy upon which Marx was most dependent. At least four of those ideas were crucial for Marx's philosophy and his critique of political economy: *dialectical development, contradiction, alienation* and *history*. Let us consider each in order. As regards dialectical development, much nonsense has been written about it, especially the textbook formula of Thesis–Antithesis–Synthesis, which is not only *not* Hegel's language but suggests a misleading mechanical operation as well. 'Wherever there is movement', Hegel wrote, 'wherever there is life, wherever anything is carried into effect in the actual world, there Dialectic is at work.'[3] Dialectic is the form of an organic process and development and in one of his clearest passages Hegel says that this form has three stages; first, a *beginning*, second, an *advance*, and, third, a *resolution*. Thus in every process of becoming – the acorn and the oak will serve as a simple illustration – there is something that goes out of itself leaving its initial form behind, grows into an environment that presents obstacles as well as support, and, if successful, realises what it had the potential to become. The oak tree is actually what, in its nature, the acorn could become. In Hegel's view all becoming exhibits this same form and he saw it at work in the development, not only of natural processes, but of the human self and self consciousness, of communities and social groups and of nations on the stage of world history. It is important to notice that Hegel laid great stress on the element of conflict and struggle accompanying all becoming, and he often expressed this as a tension of *opposites* which drives the process forward. We say, Hegel says, that man is mortal and that might seem to mean that we have two features – vitality and mortality – whereas the truth is that vitality carries within itself the germ of mortality where life turns into its opposite. Marx had his own illustration of this transformation; analysing the concept of money as a medium of exchange, Marx pointed out that we start by assigning monetary value to goods based on their capacity to meet human needs and desires, but in the course of time a reverse process sets in which stems from the abstract character of money, and we come to value things in terms of how much they cost. Marx, as may well be imagined, was very much attracted to the idea that struggle is essential to all processes of development, struggle against the obstacles standing in the way of realising some goal, and the idea figures most prominently in his insistence on the necessity of the class struggle in society as a means of bringing about its very opposite – the classless society.

The term 'contradiction', though basically a logical term, was used by Hegel in a very broad sense and Marx followed in the same vein. For Hegel everything that is has opposition in itself and thus embraces both being the same and being different, so that in this sense things are in 'contradiction'. This is especially evident when we consider self-development; in order to mature, I must leave behind my immaturity and change or become different, but I am the one who changes and at the same time remains the same self I was before. 'Contradiction', Hegel wrote, 'is the very moving principle of the world'[4] but it is not the final stage or resolution because it has itself to be overcome. There is one form of contradiction or discrepancy which is more important than any other for Hegel since it concerns the basic principle of his idealism. In his view it is necessary to distinguish between what something is in its immediate existence and what it essentially is or its truth. Thus, for example, if we have before us someone who is a statesman as distinct from being a doctor or a journalist, but who seems to fall far short of the ideal of what a statesman should be, we are inclined to say that, although he is indeed a statesman, he is no 'real' statesman.

Marx fastened upon this idea of contradiction and used it as a critical weapon in his attack on the system of bourgeois capitalism. The entire system, he declared, stands in one great contradiction; human beings as creatures of reason and freedom are to be treated, not as things to be used, but as persons of worth and dignity. In the economic system he was attacking, however, the workers are exploited and deprived of the full value of their labour and in the process are reduced to objects or commodities. The contradiction is between their immediate existence in poverty and their value as members of the human race entitled to dignity and decent living conditions. Marx added another dimension to contradiction with his idea of ideology, or the deceptive masking by those in authority of special interest and privilege behind universal 'ideals' of justice, equality and freedom. Thus there is contradiction between what the situation actually is and the way it is represented by those in power. As we shall see in connection with the discussion about the conception of history, Marx believed that these contradictions in society would *inevitably* work themselves out in resolutions through the dialectic at work in the historical order. It is difficult to exaggerate the appeal of a revolutionary vision that claims to have a supposedly necessary march of history on its side.

The idea of alienation plays a greater role in Marx's thought than it does in Hegel's, but its roots are, nevertheless, to be found in the latter's analysis of human consciousness in relation to the structure of society. As we have seen, all development for Hegel is the coming into actuality of what was there before but only in germ. Since, however, development always means the overcoming of obstacles and thus involves change – if I am to grow I can do so only by going beyond what I was before – the key question is whether I can retain my identity in the sense of becoming what I essentially am, or whether I lose myself in the process and thus become 'alien' to myself. According to Hegel, there are factors both in myself and my society which make for the possibility that I become separated from my true self, the mark of alienation. To understand the meaning of alienation in relation to society, it is necessary to take into account Hegel's overcoming of the Cartesian tradition in his view of self-consciousness. Descartes' famous *cogito* is such that each individual is aware of the 'I' in solitude and *without relation to any other ego* or to the society in which he or she exists. Hegel, on the contrary, traced the development of self-consciousness as a thoroughly social affair; I come to the consciousness of myself through mutual relations with others. I do not first have a secure apprehension of my own self and then somehow extend that to include others; on the contrary, I come to a realisation of myself as this individual in the first instance through a process of mutual recognition that already includes my interaction with other persons. Going further, Hegel was able to show that the type of self-consciousness we have is intimately connected with the kind of society in which we live. The correlation between human self-consciousness and the state of the entire political economy in which it develops was made central by Marx and it provided him with a powerful critical tool with which he could support his claim that the socio-economic system of nineteenth-century Europe had brought about alienation or a false consciousness in which human beings are separated from their true nature.

It is in these terms that one must understand what Marx says about the forms of alienation, including alienated labour, and his attack on religion as the source of alienation at the most basic level. We shall consider these forms in more detail in connection with what I see as Marx's diagnosis of the human predicament; it is helpful, however, to take note of the basic concept itself. All forms of alienation share in an estrangement or displacement wherein the

human person or some particular human capacity becomes something other than what it essentially is, which means what it can
become. Human beings, says Marx, are not merely natural beings
since all belong to the human species, persons not objects; in the
political economy, however, the labourer is reduced to a *commodity*
and is thus alienated from his or her essential humanity.

The fourth concept in Marx's debt to Hegel is found in the idea of
history. Hegel did much to establish in the nineteenth century the
idea of of history, not as in the past a succession of static epochs –
'ages of the world' – but as a dynamic continuum of events brought
about by great individuals and nations through struggle and passion leading to novel outcomes. Unlike Nature, which Hegel saw as
a quiet development of forms in time, history is made in the tensions and conflicts of human self-consciousness and human interests. For Hegel, history has its own dialectic and, in appropriating
the biblical idea of Providence, he declared that the true aim of
history is the realisation of freedom on a universal scale. Hegel's
well-known formula for this development states that in the Ori-
ental world, only one is free – the despot – in the Graeco-Roman
world, some are free, and in the modern world, all are free. Since,
however, the third stage is still in the making, Hegel modified that
to read, all *can* be free. As was noted earlier, Hegel was less sanguine about the *necessity* attaching to this process than Marx who
was wont to speak of the 'iron laws of history' which would inevitably bring about the abolition of classes and the overcoming of
special interests standing athwart the achievement of universal
human equality and justice.

Before turning directly to Marx's thought, note must be taken of
the most fundamental point at which Marx diverged from Hegel, a
divergence so sharp in Marx's mind that he described it in ironic
terms by saying that he was standing Hegel on his head. The point
is, of course, that Hegel called his position 'Absolute Idealism' and,
in countering Hegel's outlook, Marx described his revolutionary
critique as 'materialism', but of a dialectical sort. Hegel's 'idealism' –
the term can be misleading here – consists in the priority given to
reason and to the power of what he called the 'Idea' which surprisingly enough, is very much like a self-specifying system such as the
genetic code in which the specific features of an organism develop
from the whole of which they are parts. This sort of idealism has
nothing to do with the belief that the things and events of the world
are not 'real' but only figments of the 'mind'. It means instead that

reality is shot through with reason in much the same sense that the ancient Greek philosophers spoke of all things being under the control of *Nous*.

By contrast, Marx, not unlike Kierkegaard and the later philosophers of existence, revolted against this rationalism in the name of actual existence and called his philosophy 'materialism' by which he did *not* mean that reality is composed of bits of stuff in the fashion of Hobbes or Feuerbach, but rather the primacy of the historical, socio-economic situation in which people actually live, Marx, to be sure, had his own need of ideas – his vision is loaded with them – but he saw ideas as neither prevenient nor supervenient, but as developing out of the interaction between individuals and groups in society and between competing interests in a system where workers must struggle to gain the means of subsistence. What Marx meant by calling his materialism 'dialectical' as opposed to 'old-fashioned' materialism, can be seen from his own simple illustration; the old materialism thought it sufficient to put idealism in its place simply by insisting that 'before one can think, one must first eat', whereas Marx, while he did not deny this dictum, insisted that 'in order to eat, one must think', that is to say that to obtain the means of subsistence requires ingenuity and thought. In short, dialectical materialism recognises the interplay between thought and the historical situation, while regarding the latter as the matrix from which all thought arises.

One of the striking facts about Marxism, one that shows how well suited it is to serve as a quasi-religion, is the way in which it manifests the pattern previously described as the structure of religion – diagnosis of the human predicament in the light of an ideal expressing human fulfilment, location of what separates human beings from that ideal and finding a means of deliverance through which the separation is overcome. The ideal to which Marx appealed in making his diagnosis of the human condition in the world is akin to the ideal espoused by Humanism – the individual as a *human* and *humane* being living under humane social conditions. Before we can say what this means in detail, it is necessary to deal with the claim made by some Marxists that Marx regarded as idle and 'speculative' all discussions about the nature of man as such. That this is not so can be shown by many statements in his *Economic and Philosophical Manuscripts*, not to mention *Capital*. One of the best philosophical interpreters of Marx, Gajo Petrovic; is emphatic on this point. 'But nothing is more false', he wrote, 'than the assumption that Marx condemned discussions about man in general.'[5] The fact is that Marx was thoroughly involved in the question of human nature and in the need to have some conception of what an *un*alienated or emancipated human being would be like in order to make his critical diagnosis of man's distorted existence in the industrial world of nineteenth-century Europe. There is an even deeper reason why Marx had to develop a picture of essential human nature and it stems from his critique of religion. 'To be radical', Marx wrote,

> is to grasp things by the root. But for man the root is man himself ... The criticism of religion ends with the doctrine that *man is the supreme being for man*. IT ends, therefore, with the *categorical imperative to overthrow all those conditions* in which man is an abased, enslaved abandoned, contemptible being – conditions which can hardly be better described than in the exclamation of a Frenchman on the occasion of a proposed tax upon dogs: 'Wretched dogs! they want to treat you like men![6]

We shall return to Marx's criticism of religion; for the moment it is important to see that, if man is to be the supreme being for man, the standard for judgement surely cannot be found in the abased and enslaved man, but must reside in some ideal conception of human existence. What, then, is Marx's theory of man in general and how does it serve as a touchstone for his diagnosis of what there is which stands in the way of an ideal human fulfilment? These questions are obviously intertwined with each other; in answering them one must draw both directly on what Marx says about essential human nature, and what is said by implication in the diagnosis itself. Petrovic, paraphrasing Marx, writes, 'To ask, What is man? means to ask what it is by virtue of which man is that integral being that differs essentially from everything else that exists.'[7] Marx was critical of the many attempts to define man in terms of some special property or sphere which he inhabits such as we find in the classical definition of man as a rational animal or as a political animal, and later, as a tool-making animal. All these traits, and indeed many others, belong to human beings, but no one of them, nor even a so-called 'sum' of such traits captures the essence of being human. As Marx was aware, the relations between the domains in which we exist – economic, moral, political, artistic, etc. – do not remain unchanged forever, but differ from period to period, and hence he sought for some more fundamental way of characterising what it means to be human. The problem here is, of course, not new nor is it confined to defining the human, since it appears whenever an attempt is made to indicate the 'essence' of anything; one can reject any feature proposed as being too narrow, abstract or not 'fundamental' enough, but if one is to say more than that to be human is to be human, it will be necessary to select some feature as definitive. Marx did just that, and declared that the relationship of human beings to the world and to themselves is best expressed by saying that to be human is to be the being of *praxis*; activity captures the essence. Among other reasons for the choice of this emphasis of Marx's part was his leaning in an 'existentialist' direction which means leaning away from the idea of a *fixed* essence that unfolds in time and toward dynamism, creativity and power. Since, however, activity is peculiar to all animals, it was necessary for Marx to say what is distinctive of human activity. 'The animal,' Marx wrote, 'is one with its life activity. It does not distinguish the activity from itself. It is *its activity*. But man makes his life activity itself an object of his will and consciousness. He has a conscious life activity. It is not a determination with which he is completely identified. Conscious life activity distinguishes man from the life activity of animals.'[8] Petrovic is right in saying that this attempt at characterising human activity is valid as far as it goes, but that in so far as consciousness is the only distinguishing feature, we seem to be merely reinstating the idea that man is the rational animal. However, that Marx was aware of the need for something more is suggested by his previous statement that activity 'is not a determination with which he is completely identified'. There must then be other relations between human beings and their activity than the fact that it is conscious.

Here still another idea of Hegel's comes into play and it is at least as important as those previously mentioned. In the *Phenomenology* Hegel has a well-known section in which he speaks about man's appropriation of the world, not merely knowing or contemplating it, but in mastering it to serve human ends, and in *work* where some tangible product results which expresses the person who produces it. The product made represents the objective realisation of the maker and he or she looks at it and sees a mirror of themselves or what they can actually accomplish in the world. Marx put this idea to good use as we see in the following two passages from the *Economic and Philosophical Manuscripts*, the first of which further specifies the nature of human activity, while the second focuses on labour and its relation to what he calls man's 'species being'.[9] 'It is just in his work upon the objective world', Marx says,

> that man really proves himself as a *species-being*. This production is his active species-life. . . . By means of it nature appears as *his* work and his reality. The object of labor is, therefore, the *object-ification of man's species-life*; for he no longer reproduces himself merely intellectually, as in consciousness, but actively and in a real sense, and he sees his own reflection in a world which he has constructed. (Bottomore, p. 128)

What distinguishes human activity from that of animals is not only the fact of its being conscious, but also its role in objectifying life through the things that are the result of work and the manipulation of nature.

Marx made a significant addition to Feuerbach's concept as we see in the second passage. 'Man is a species-being,' Marx writes,

> not only in the sense that he makes the community . . . his object both practically and theoretically, but also . . . in the sense that he treats himself as the present, living species, as a *universal* and consequently free being . . . The universality of man appears in practice in the universality which makes the whole of nature into his inorganic body: (1) as a direct means of life; and equally (2) as the material object and instrument of his life activity. (Bottomore, p. 126)

Hence, for Marx, the consciousness of a species-being is not only the awareness of belonging to mankind as a species, but also the awareness of being free and at the same time the master of nature through work.

What, we may ask, have the ideas of activity, labour and the species-being added to Marx's conception of the human being? The main feature is the emphasis on universal creativity, the ability to make things and to transform the face of nature. Creativity, how-ever, does not stop there; not unlike Nietzsche later on, Marx begins to talk about man creating *himself*, and this step is a consequence of, on the one hand, denying that man has a fixed essence other than activity, and, on the other, taking *history* seriously in the sense of the realisation of human potentialities in the future. The point has sometimes been expressed by saying that the human being is to be understood not so much in terms of having a nature, as in having a social history through which man creates himself. There is a most instructive passage in Marx's third Manuscript of 1844 which confirms the point. 'Since, however, for socialist man', Marx wrote,

> the *whole of what is called world history* is nothing but the creation of man by human labor, and the emergence of nature for man, he, therefore, has the evident and irrefutable proof of his *self-creation*, of his own *origins*. (Bottomore, p. 166)

This view has important repercussions for Marx's treatment of religion and, in fact, it adds a new dimension to what we may call his standard critique of religion. According to that critique, man sought a supernatural being in a fantastic heaven, but what he found was only a reflection of himself which is not his true being, but only a semblance. The truth is that '*man makes religion*; religion does not make man'. Religion is man's self-consciousness, but only so long as he has not yet found himself. The abolition of religion with its illusory happiness is at the same time a call to find true happiness.

> The criticism of religion disillusions man so that he will think, act and fashion reality as a man who has lost his illusions and regained his reason; so that he will revolve about himself as his own true sun. Religion is only the illusory sun about which man revolves so long as he does not revolve about himself.[10]

Once the idea, expressed in the foregoing quotation, of man as a natural being and of nature as a human reality have become evident in practical life – Marx even says 'in sense experience' – the critique of religion can be carried one step further. First, the quest for an *alien* being above man and nature becomes impossible in practice, because for Marx, such a quest is an affirmation of the unreality of both. Second, atheism, which is the denial of this unreality, is no longer meaningful, says Marx, since atheism seeks to negate God by affirming the *existence of man*. This step is now no longer necessary since, so to speak, we already have the existence of man evident in practical life. 'Socialism', Marx continues,

> no longer requires such a roundabout method;' it begins from the *theoretical* and *practical sense perception* of man and nature as

essential beings. It is positive human *self-consciousness*, no longer
a self consciousness attained through the negation of religion.
(Bottomore, p. 167)

The underlying thesis can be stated even more directly and even
without the detour through self-consciousness: man can be, only if
God is not; if God exists, man does not. It is of the utmost interest
that for Marx, as later for Sartre, the eclipse of God comes about by
the identification of man with freedom coupled with the belief that,
if God is admitted, freedom and even man himself would be nulli-
fied. If, moreover, human beings are to create themselves, the role
of God would seem to have been pre-empted.

Having gained an understanding of Marx's conception of man as
a species being who through life-activity (*praxis*) constructs the
world and creates himself in the historical order, we must ask,
What does Marx think is wrong about the actual human situation, what stands in the way of man's becoming what he should be
which is to say, his essential nature? Beyond that we have still to
ask, What is the means of overcoming the obstacles that separate
man from his true self and of realising this essential human being?
The pattern, it should be noted, is that of diagnosis of the flaw in the
actual situation as seen from the perspective of the ideal, followed
by the identification of the means of deliverance or emancipation.
This pattern correlates with the pattern manifested in what have
been called the religions proper.

The answer to our first question is found in what has come to be
known as the four forms of alienation wherein human beings are
said to have been estranged from themselves. In considering these
forms, we shall also have occasion to ask whether for Marx, alienation is a permanent feature of the human situation as distinct from
being merely a phase in history where the conditions for alienation
prevail. Although Marx differentiated the forms or 'characteristics'
of alienation, it is clear that all are basically the alienation of man
from himself. Starting with what he calls a 'contemporary economic fact', Marx sees the first alienation as the estrangement of the
worker from the product that he or she produces. 'The *devaluation*
of the human world increases', Marx claims,

in direct relation with the *increase in value* of the world of things.
Labour does not only create goods; it also produces itself and the
worker as a *commodity*.

The labour that is embodied in what the worker makes becomes a physical thing and 'the more the worker expends himself in work the more powerful becomes the world of objects which he creates in face of himself, the poorer he becomes in his inner life, and the less he belongs to himself' (Bottomore, p. 122). What is embodied in the product of labour no longer belongs to the labourer. 'The *alienation* of the worker', Marx contends, 'in his product means not only that his labour becomes an object, assumes an *external* existence, but that it exists independently, *outside* himself, and *alien* to him, and that it stands opposed to him as an autonomous power' (Bottomore, pp. 122–3). The second form of alienation is implicit in the first; alienation appears not only in the product or result but in the process as well, so that the activity of production is itself alien to the producer since the work he does belongs not to himself, but to someone else. Marx summarises these two forms as follows:

> What constitutes the alienation of labour? First, that the work is *external* to the worker, that it is not part of his nature; and that, consequently, he does not fulfil himself in his work but denies himself. . . . The worker, therefore, feels himself at home only during his leisure time, whereas at work he feels homeless. . . . Finally, the external character of work for the worker is shown by the fact that it is not his own work but work for someone else, that in work he does not belong to himself but to another person. (Bottomore, pp. 124–5)

Here we see the dialectic of opposites at work; the individual feels herself to be acting spontaneously only in her animal functions – eating, drinking, dressing, procreating – while in her human functions she is reduced to an animal. The animal becomes human and the human becomes animal.

There are, for Marx, two further forms of alienation stemming from the previous two – man is alienated both from the species and from other men, His idea in the former case is that alienated labour turns species life which distinguishes man from animals into something alien because each individual sees that life and activity merely as a *means* for his or her *individual* existence and this leads directly to the fourth form which is alienation from other men or women. When man confronts himself, says Marx, he also confronts *other* men and with the result that they are as alien to him as he is to his work and himself. Marx sees the condition of alienated

labour as filled with contradictions in the sense previously set
forth. If, he says, the product of labour does not belong to the
worker, it must belong to someone else, and, since neither nature
nor the gods can be made responsible, it must be that 'only man
himself can be this alien power over men'. It turns out that the
producer 'creates the domination of the non-producer over production and its product. As he alienates his own activity, so he bestows
upon the stranger an activity that is not his own' (Bottomore,
p. 131). The culmination of the process for Marx is the derivation of
private property, as we see in the following:

> Through alienated labor the worker creates the relation of an-
> other man, who does not work and is outside the work process,
> to this labour. The relation of the worker to work also produces
> the relation of the capitalist (or whatever one likes to call the lord
> of labour) to work. *Private property* is, therefore, the product, the
> necessary result, of *alienated labour*, of the external relation of the
> worker to nature and to himself. (p. 131)

We need not pursue this dialectic further since to do so would
involve political and economic considerations not directly relevant
for Marx's diagnosis of the human situation. More important is the
question whether alienation belongs to the structure of human
existence or is only a phenomenon characteristic of one historical
stage in human development. The answer to this question is complicated by the fact that 'Marxism' came to include the ideas of
Engels as well as Marx. Engels believed that there was an original
non-alienated human condition and he developed the idea in *The
Origin of the Family*, but Marx seems not to have accepted this view.
The position most frequently taken by Marx was that man has been
alienated *thus far*, but that he need not remain so, and indeed no
other position would be consistent with his programme for de-
alienation through communism. Petrovic correctly sums up Marx's
view by pointing to the way in which he contrasts the present
situation with that of the projected future. 'Marx', Petrovic writes,
'clearly contrasts the contemporary and the future society as the
alienated and the non-alienated one, as the inhuman and the really
human one – all of which means that Marx regarded alienation as a
historically transient characteristic of man, a phenomenon characteristic of all previous history, but not necessarily of the future'
(Petrovic, p. 88). The point is of great importance because it shows

that for Marx what must be overcome, what human beings are to be delivered from, is tractable in the sense that at least in principle the transcendence of alienation is possible and, presumably, through the effort of presently alienated human beings if man is indeed to become the sun around which he revolves.

Marxism thus joins hands with Humanism in the belief that man is his own measure and end and that whatever evils beset human beings are to be dispelled, if at all, solely through human effort. Marxism, however, has a more sharply focused conception of man's estrangement from himself than is to be found in Humanism which is by comparison 'one dimensional' in the sense that what needs to be attacked are just so many evils in the world – error, ignorance, intolerance, repression, illusion, including that of religion, but there is no sense of man's being radically alienated from his true nature. Marx can speak of man's existence or actual situation at the time he was writing, as being in conflict with, or in contradiction to, his essential nature and his position is 'two-dimensional' in that the resolution envisaged – de-alienation – is the recovery of a being from which alienated man was separated. Humanism, largely because it has assumed so many forms, has no such central focus. There is, however, no need to press that point since Marx has given his own account of the connection between his view and humanism. 'In the same way', he wrote,

> atheism as the annulment of God is the emergence of theoretical humanism, and communism as the annulment of private property is the vindication of real human life as man's property. The latter is also the emergence of practical humanism. (Petrovic, pp. 161–2)

Although Marx was much concerned about the negation of religion, in numerous places we find him claiming that the humanism that is dependent on the negation of God is not what he calls the 'self-originating-*positive* humanism' that emerges from the annulment of private property.[11]

So much, then, for Marx's diagnosis of the human predicament. From that analysis we have a fairly clear picture of what needs to be achieved. In his discussion of what he called the 'third phase' of communism, Marx speaks of the abolition of man's self-alienation, or the return of man to himself and the recovery of what had been lost. Religion, the family, the state, science, art, etc., he says, are merely special modes of production and 'the positive supersession of *private property*, as the appropriation of *human* life, is therefore the *positive* supersession of all alienation, and the return of man from religion, the family, the state, etc., to his *human*, i.e., *social* life' (Petrovic, p. 163). The overarching goal that defines Marx's vision is the recovery of human life as human in and through a humanistic society. How, then, is this to be achieved? What is the means of delivery?

It should be obvious at the outset that no simple answer can be given to these questions. Even if Marx frequently writes that the abolition of private property is the key to the resolution, the picture is far more complex than that and the main reason is that whatever recovery there is for human beings must take place through re-arrangements in society and within an historical order which means that it is necessary to take account of the nature of historical change and how it can be brought about. Marx had one grand strategy in this regard, one he derived from Hegel's analysis of development, or what he called 'becoming'. Every process according to Hegel, that results in the realisation of a goal must begin with something actual – an organism, a group, a society – which has in it the real possibility or the requisite conditions for bringing about the result. In Hegel's view, the need for an actuality containing real possibilities is felt in all historical development, but it has special relevance to human efforts to realise some ideal, some future state of affairs such as Marx's vision of a society in which the class struggle would be overcome and social classes would themselves disappear. As Hegel pointed out, ideals become no more than wish or fantasy unless there is already extant in the present, actual situation the conditions which make the realisation of that ideal a real possibility. Those conditions are not brought about by human effort alone, but, when present, they can be made the material in and through which woman's activity is able to bring about the desired transformation of society.

Marx, as is clear from his critique of Hegel's *Philosophy of Right*, took all these ideas very seriously and developed his own conception of how his ideal, both for the individual and society, could be realised. Consider the ingredients Marx envisioned; first, there is the Marxian individual who is a being of *praxis* or transforming activity, second, there is the existence of conflicting interests between classes in society – Marx often expressed this as the opposition between *property* owners and *propertyless* workers – and, third, there is the historical process itself which, as Hegel had repeatedly insisted, moves in the direction of realising freedom for all people. With these ingredients in the actual situation, Marx set out to show how the overcoming of alienation and the establishment of a human society could be accomplished.

In considering the political situation prevailing in Germany in the early nineteenth century, Marx came to distinguish between a *political* revolution where one section of civil society emancipates itself and dominates the others, while leaving 'the pillars of the building standing', and a *radical* revolution aimed at universal human emancipation. Reflecting further on the role a class might play in a radical revolution, Marx formed his key idea which we find expressed in the following passage:

> No class in civil society can play this part [i.e., emancipating the whole society] unless it can arouse, in itself and in the masses, a moment of enthusiasm in which it associates and mingles with the society at large, identifies itself with it, and is felt and recognized as the *general representative* of this society. Its aims and interests must genuinely be the aims and interests of society itself, of which it becomes in reality the social head and heart. It is only in the name of general interests that a particular class can claim general supremacy. (Bottomore, pp. 55–6).

Here we see Marx beginning with the idea of an *actual* class in society which, if it succeeds in representing the interests of the whole society, can serve as the means of revolutionary transformation. Since, however, as Marx says, 'revolutionary energy and consciousness of its own power' in this class will not suffice, it must be endowed with something more. The 'something more' – and here Marx shows clearly that the class he has in mind is the *working proletariat* – is found in the fact that this class has been subjected to infinite evils and oppression, the victim of the opposing classes. 'For a *popular revolution* and the *emancipation of a particular class* in civil society to coincide', Marx writes,

> for *one* class to represent the whole of society, another class must concentrate in itself all the evils of society, a particular class must embody and represent a general obstacle and limitation. A particular social sphere must be regarded as the *notorious crime* of the whole society, so that emancipation from this sphere appears as

a general emancipation. For *one* class to be the liberating class *par excellence*, it is necessary that another class should be openly the oppressing class. (Bottomore, p. 56).

It is important to notice that although the proletariat form a class among others in an alienated society, for Marx that class represents the universal interests of *humanity* against all other special or limited interests and in liberating itself from oppression it liberates the entire society in overcoming the existence of classes as such. If, moreover, history is the story of liberty, the proletariat in representing the universal interest of a free and human society, has history on its side. As noted previously, Marx was more sanguine than Hegel about the *inevitability* of the historical process itself, but especially the necessary working out of the class struggle supposed to result in the classless society.

We now have before us a picture of Marxism and Marx's programme sufficient for understanding why it is fitted to serve as a quasi-religion. There is the vision of a new society and a new human being and both serve as the criteria for a diagnosis and prophetic critique[12] of existing society; there is the phenomenon of alienation in all its forms as what separates human beings from their true selves; there is a form of deliverance through the proletariat's role in the class struggle and in the historical development through which the class that alone represents the interests of humanity and freedom will bring into being the new society that is beyond alienation. Like Humanism, Marxism sees humanity as its own end so that the supreme object of loyalty and devotion is to the cause of realising the society in which human possibilities can come to fruition. There is, of course, no acknowledgement of any transcendent reality in the properly religious sense, although it is highly significant that Marx, in describing the proletariat as the group against which universal crimes have been committed, endows this group with all possible virtues – honesty, industriousness, loyalty and courage – and thus seems to hold them exempt from the vices that attach to their oppressors. There is an undeniable apocalyptic element in Marxism, the vision of the triumph of the good over the evil, and this remains intact despite disagreements among Marxists about the extent to which the goal is to be realised in the actual course of history. The hope engendered in the disinherited by this cosmic vision of redemption has proved to be one of the main motives behind the spread of Marxism throughout the world. What could be more compelling to the victims of poverty and injustice than a gospel that promises to afflict the comfortable and comfort the afflicted?

Having considered, albeit briefly, what we may call the theoretical grounds for calling Marxism a quasi-religion, it is time to turn to the evidence furnished by the experiences of a number of well-known intellectuals for whom Marxism as a philosophy and in some cases membership in the Communist Party assumed for them the form of a personal faith demanding unconditional commitment.[13] The reflections of such figures as Arthur Koestler, Ignazio Silone, André Gide, Richard Wright and others aim at explaining what it was about Communism that first captured their allegiance and why they came to abandon it as, in the very revealing title of their book, *The God that Failed*.[14] These reflections are, of course, tempered with hindsight and a sense of disillusion, but the authors have sought to minimise their feelings at the time of writing in order to recapture what factors led them to embrace Communism in the first place. As the Editor points out in the Introduction, although the authors have quite different personalities, they came together in having lost faith in Democracy, on the one hand, and in believing that Communism was better equipped to defeat Fascism, on the other. 'Their conversion', he writes, 'in fact, was rooted in despair – a despair of Western values' by which they meant a belief in automatic progress, in a steadily expanding capitalism and the abolition of power politics.[15] On the positive side, the intellectual attraction of Marxism was in its critique of liberal illusions; progress is not automatic, capitalism is caught in the cycle of 'boom and bust', injustice and discrimination do not disappear 'through history', and, given the realities of human nature and the make-up of nations, it is naive to think of doing away with 'power politics'. Much more, however, was involved than these intellectual considerations; there was the appeal to sacrifice for the cause. As Richard Crossman puts it, 'the idea of an active comradeship of struggle – involving personal sacrifice and abolishing differences of class and race – has had a compulsive power in every Western democracy' (p. 6). One can see in these reflections by former Communists a dialectic born of the burden of individual conscience and the weight of freedom wherein it becomes possible for a person to surrender spiritual freedom and even truth if that person becomes convinced of being the servant of a higher purpose that, paradoxically, demands everything and offers nothing. It is analogous to the religious surrender – what James called in the *Varieties* the 'letting go' – where the self consigns itself, as it were, to the hands of a higher power that works within, and relieves the person from the awesome task of being the sole determiner of its own destiny.

Arthur Koestler's account – 'from the psychologist's point of view' – of how little difference there is between a 'revolutionary' and a 'traditionalist' faith makes quite clear why Marxism became a powerful quasi-religion. 'All true faith', he writes,

> Is uncompromising, radical, purist; hence the true traditionalist is always a revolutionary zealot in conflict with pharisaic society, with the lukewarm corrupters of the creed. And vice versa: the revolutionary's Utopia, which in appearance represents a complete break with the past, is always modeled on some image of the lost Paradise, of a legendary Golden Age. The classless Communist society, according to Marx and Engels, was to be a revival, at the end of the dilectical spiral, of the primitive Communist society which stood at the beginning. Thus all true faith involves a revolt against the believer's social environment, and the projection into the future of an ideal derived from a remote past. (p. 16)

If we assume, as I believe we must, that a 'traditionalist' faith means an historical religion, in this case the Judeo-Christian tradition, the parallel with Marxism could not be more clear. And indeed Koestler unabashedly speaks of himself as having been a 'convert' to this revolutionary faith in terms reminiscent of Augustine's turn from his own vanity to the light of the God whom he described as Truth.[16] Koestler's 'confession' expresses this turn in the most vivid way. 'Tired of electrons and wave mechanics', he writes,

> I began for the first time to read Marx, Engels and Lenin in earnest. By the time I had finished with *Feuerbach* and *State and Revolution*, something had clicked in my brain which shook me like a mental explosion. To say that one had 'seen the light' is a poor description of the mental rapture which only the convert knows (regardless of what faith he has been converted to). The new light seems to pour from all directions across the skull; the whole universe falls into pattern like the stray pieces of a jigsaw puzzle assembled by magic at one stroke. There is now an answer to every question, doubts and conflicts are a matter of the tor-

tured past – a past already remote, when one had lived in dismal ignorance in the tasteless, colorless world of those who *don't know*. Nothing henceforth, can disturb the convert's inner peace and serenity – except the occasional fear of losing faith again, losing thereby what alone makes life worth living, and falling back into the outer darkness, where there is wailing and gnashing of teeth. (p. 23)

In this statement we can see the two sides of faith woven together; on one side there is the awareness of *choosing*, identifying oneself with, the new truth – Koestler had previously said 'it was not by a process of elimination that I became a communist' – and on the other side there is the strong sense of having been *grasped by* this truth as if one were chosen by it. The Marxist message was one that 'made sense' of the universe for someone who had been seriously in quest of a way out of despair over the values of Western civilisation which seemed no longer to be providing solutions for human ills, but had in fact become contributors to the perpetuation of these same ills. Koestler, moreover, clearly sees how such a faith as he had acquired concerned his whole being so that, as he says, the only fear that remained was the fear of losing faith again and of losing 'what alone makes life worth living'.

This turnabout in outlook and conviction was, however, to be only the beginning of Koestler's odyssey; his next step was to enlist in the cause by becoming a member of the Party and thus find some concrete way in which he could contribute to the realisation of the new society. As Royce pointed out on numerous occasions, loyalty and devotion to an undertaking easily degenerates into mere sentiment unless one finds or is given concrete tasks to perform in service to the cause. Koestler was to learn this lesson, but in doing so he discovered what the cost would be and what effect it would have upon his own life. It is not difficult to see that what would happen to him in the succeeding months would raise doubts in his mind about the newly found faith.

To begin with, he joined the Party when it was preparing to go underground and thus its activities would be illegal. 'The new recruit to the Party', he writes,

found himself plunged into a strange world, as if he were entering a deep-sea aquarium with its phosphorescent light and fleeting, elusive shapes. It was a world populated by people with

Christian names only – Edgars and Paulas and Ivans – without surname or address. . . . It was a paradoxical atmosphere – a blend of fraternal comradeship and mutual distrust. Its motto might have been: Love your comrade, but don't trust him an inch. (p. 29)

Almost from the beginning, Koestler became aware that such an atmosphere is more than an external environment because it meant a gradual transformation of character and the distortion of human relationships. Koestler experienced this transformation in himself as the result of the rigid thought patterns imposed by a party that regards its doctrine as infallible. 'I learned', he frankly admits,

> to distrust my mechanistic preoccupation with facts and to re-gard the world around me in the light of dialectic interpretation. It was a satisfactory and indeed blissful state; once you had assimilated the technique you were no longer disturbed by facts; they automatically took on the proper color and fell into their proper place. Both morally and logically the Party was infallible: morally, because its aims were right, that is, in accord with the Dialectic of History, and these aims justified all means; logically, because the Party was the vanguard of the Proletariat, and the Proletariat the embodiment of the active principle in History.[17]

The accommodation of fact to dialectic, as Koestler discovered, was not the end of the sacrifices required; since members of the intelligentsia could not really become members of the Proletariat, they had to limit themselves severely and were not to think, as Koestler says, 'anything which could not be understood by the dustman' (p. 49). Consequently, he continues, 'We cast off our intellectual baggage like passengers on a ship seized by panic, until it became reduced to the strictly necessary minimum of stock-phrases, dialectical clichés and Marxist quotations' (p. 49). Reconditioning of Party members did not stop at thought, but extended to language as well. The expression 'lesser evil' was taboo as was also 'spontaneous' because the theory of Permanent Revolution set forth by Trotsky – notorious as a 'revisionist' and traitor to the cause – made reference to 'spontaneous' manifestations of revolutionary class consciousness.

Being a writer of more than ordinary talent, Koestler was especially sensitive to the strictures placed on literary and artistic expression. Balzac, for example, was declared the greatest writer of all time because Lenin said he learned more about France from his novels than from all the history books. In art, Koestler tells us, the guiding principle was Revolutionary Dynamism which meant that 'a picture without a smoking factory chimney or a tractor in it was escapist' (p. 46). In music and drama, the chorus was regarded as the highest form of expression 'because it reflected a collective, as opposed to a bourgeois-individualistic, approach' (ibid.).

Koestler had gone to Russia in the summer of 1932 and he was shocked by the awesome poverty he encountered in the Ukraine, but there were always the mitigating explanations – living standards are low, but they were even lower under the Czarist regime; workers in capitalist countries are better off than those in the Soviet Union, but things will be equalised by the end of the second Five Year Plan, etc. He found himself believing that the facts must be interpreted in a 'dynamic' way and not at face value, and that distortions of all sorts were necessary for the survival of the Soviet Union in a world of enemies. 'The necessary lie', he says, 'the necessary slander; the necessary intimidation of the masses to preserve them from shortsighted errors; the necessary liquidation of a whole generation in the interest of the next – it may all sound monstrous and yet it was so easy to accept while rolling along the single track of faith' (p. 61). His was a robust faith indeed, one able not only to move mountains, but to make mountains of facts disappear. As Koestler continues his story, one can see that he was becoming increasingly sceptical about how much 'reconditioning' he could accept and yet, as he says, some events and inner rationalisations helped him to continue and delay the 'crack-up'. One such event, the turnabout in policy announced at the meeting of the Comintern in 1934, afforded Koestler 'a second honeymoon with the Party' (p. 63). The new policy, a total negation of the past, called for scrapping revolutionary slogans, being done with talk about the class struggle and the dictatorship of the Proletariat, and replacing them with a brand-new programme called the 'Popular Front for Peace and Against Fascism'. Still under the spell of his faith, Koestler seems to have been able to accept this new line as something positive in intent, even though he was aware of how much it made it necessary to falsify the past. The new 'truth' was that Communists – even the name was to be dropped – *never* advocated violence and revolution, these were slanderous inventions of reactionary warmongers, now 'we're just simple, honest, peace-loving anti-Fascists and defenders of democracy' (p. 62).

It is important to take note of the powerful hold that the Party had over him. Though, Koestler says, we had blinkers on, we were not blind, and it was impossible not to see that all was far from well. The restraining belief was that the Party could not be changed except from the inside because it is not like a club nor is it an ordinary sort of party. 'You could resign', Koestler writes,

> from a club and from the ordinary sort of party if its policy no longer suited you; but the Communist Party was something entirely different: it was the vanguard of the Proletariat, the incarnation of the will of History itself (p. 65). If you left the Party you abandoned any chance of influencing its future. Hence the only course was to risk all on the course of history – 'to remain inside, shut your mouth tight, swallow your bile and wait for the day when, after the defeat of the enemy and the victory of World Revolution, Russia and the Comintern were ready to become democratic institutions' (p. 66). Until this apocalyptic time arrives, one had 'to play the game' . . . it was the price you had to pay for being allowed to continue feeling useful, and thus keep your perverted self-respect. (p. 66)

No one can fail to see how decidedly these ingredients of Marxism had assumed for Koestler and others the character of religious symbols demanding from an individual a total and unconditional commitment. *The* Party is more than a party; it is, in fact, more like a church eliciting absolute loyalty from its members and providing a means of fulfilment for the deep-seated human need, as Koestler says 'to continue feeling useful' even under such wretched conditions.[18] The same holds for the other capitalised expressions – History, World Revolution, the Proletariat – each of which becomes endowed with more than human power and is regarded as one of the determiners of human destiny. 'History' is not simply a mundane order of events, it is *the* medium through which the new society is to come about and it moves inexorably towards this end. The 'Proletariat' does not mean merely groups of workers, but is the name of *the* class that bears the cause of Humanity on its back, a cosmic force which is to redeem all human beings. 'World Revolution' is not the name of an uprising to be assigned a date in a history book, but the apocalyptic event that ushers in the classless society, the culmination of the Marxist vision. We are here in a world of symbols or bearers of meaning which unite thought and

passion, evoking loyalty, discipline, sacrifice – all in the name of
a cause.

Here it is certainly not out of place to point out that Communism
has not been without its own quasi-religious symbols intended to
evoke loyalty and to focus enthusiasm on its heroes and its ideology. We are familiar with the statues of Lenin, the huge pictures of
Stalin in Russia and of Castro in Cuba, and the 'sacred' days in May
and October. Mao Zedong's Cultural Revolution in China, however, seems to have gone much further not only in attacking religion but in seeking to replace it. Julia Ching records that in the 'bad
years' of the Revolution domestic shrines in homes were destroyed
and pictures of Mao were put in their place, red flags were used to
replace crosses in Christian churches, Bibles were burned and busts
of Mao placed in the centre of houses of worship. Nor was this all;
'During the Cultural Revolution', she writes,

> people were made to demonstrate their devotion to Mao Zedong,
> the great leader, rather than to God or Buddha. Throughout the
> country, a new liturgy was carried out as people paid respect
> to their Mao portraits mornings and evenings, seeking daily
> instructions from him in a quasi-religious manner . . . . Thus
> Maoism became a surrogate religion offering a new faith, elucid-
> ated in the Little Red Book, Mao images, lapel buttons, posters,
> songs, drama and even 'liturgy'.[19]

According to Ching, there was even something akin to a sacred
space – Tian'anmen Square – in which the rituals of Maoism took
place. Marxism has always stood at the border of religion, far more
so than naturalistic Humanism ever could, but Marxism cannot
cross that border because in its 'scientific' pretensions it limits itself
to finite and secular things. The most it can do is to raise humanity,
history, revolution to an *absolute* level, to a degree of ultimacy
which in the end finite realities are unable to bear. Hence Marxism
remains a quasi-religion, one that diagnoses the ills of human
society and prophesies a deliverance which the Party, the class
struggle and the dialectic of history cannot fulfil. This we can see
in the final chapter of Koestler's involvement with the Party when
he decided that the 'God' had indeed 'failed'. Captured by Franco's
troops when a correspondent with the Republican Army, Koestler
spent four months in Spanish prisons during which he was mostly
in solitary confinement and convinced that he was to be shot.

Fortunately, the British Government intervened and he was unexpectedly released. In retrospect, he sought to express the 'different kind of reality' with which he became acquainted in these dire experiences and which as he writes, 'had altered my outlook and values . . . so profoundly and unconsciously that during the first days of freedom I was not even aware of it' (p. 67). He knew fear, not so much of death, but of torture and personal humiliation, and he knew pity – 'for the little Andalusian and Catalan peasants whom I heard crying and calling for their *madres* when they were led out at night to face the firing squad . . .' (pp. 67–8). Koestler found the lesson he had learned so profound that putting it into words seemed to result merely in commonplaces. The principles involved, nevertheless, stand out with great clarity: human beings are real and mankind is an abstraction; men are not units 'in operations of political arithmetic'; the end can be said to justify the means only within very narrow limits; ethics is *not* a matter of social utility and, most important, charity is not a *petitbourgeois* sentiment, 'but the gravitational force which keeps civilization in its orbit' (p. 68). In summary, Koestler declares that every one of these statements was 'incompatible with the Communist faith which I held' (ibid.).

Under these circumstances, Koestler knew that his involvement with the Party must end and he prefaced his resignation with a speech about the situation in Spain.[20] The speech focused on three phrases which, as he says, would appear to normal people as platitudes, but to Communists as a 'declaration of war'. These are the phrases: 'No movement, party or person can claim the privilege of infallibility'; 'Appeasing the enemy is as foolish as persecuting the friend who pursues your own aim by a different road'; and, a quotation from Thomas Mann, 'A harmful truth is better than a useful lie'.

The odyssey of the Italian writer, Ignazio Silone, is especially illuminating because here we have a person steeped in the Roman Catholic faith, but who for almost a decade, transferred that commitment to the Communist Party, and he describes in the most personal terms what that sacrifice meant to him. Born in the Abruzzi Apennines, Silone saw at first hand what a hard life of poverty and injustice means, especially to a person with a Christian conscience. In 1921 Silone took part in the founding of the Italian Communist Party, having come to believe that through it some semblance of the Kingdom of God on earth might be achieved. 'For me to join the Party of the Proletarian Revolution', he writes, 'was not just a simple matter of signing up with a political organization; it meant a conversion, a complete dedication' (p. 98). and he goes on to describe what happened to his 'Middle Ages' faith from which came his aspiration to revolt in the process: it 'was shaken to their foundations, as though by an earthquake. Everything was thrown into the melting pot. . . . Life, death, love, good, evil, truth, all changed their meaning or lost it altogether' (ibid.). Like Koestler, Silone testifies to the awesome presence and power of the Party – 'The Party became family, school, church, barracks; the world that lay beyond it was to be destroyed and built anew' (p. 99), and he likens the manner in which the individual is incorporated into the collective to the practices of some religious orders and military schools. Again, like Koestler's experience, Silone found that the more dangers and sacrifices were involved, the firmer the bond with the Party became, for every personal sacrifice meant a contribution to 'collective redemption' (ibid.).

For a variety of reasons – authoritarianism, fanaticism, opportunism, distortion of truth – Silone came to the realisation that he could no longer continue as a member of the Party, but what is most striking about his decision to leave is that it was as traumatic as his enlisting in the first place. 'The day I left the Communist Party', he writes, 'was a very sad one for me, it was like a day of deep mourning, the mourning for my lost youth' (p. 113), and he goes on to express how difficult it was to free himself from the deeply ingrained experience of an underground organisation – 'Something of it remains and leaves a mark on the character which lasts all one's life' (ibid.). We have here striking testimony to the crucial fact that the Party demanded and received the whole *being* of the person. Just as both Koestler and Silone described the Party as something far more than a political organisation, both realised that it engaged their lives at a level far deeper than politics can reach. The Party and its avowed aim of world revolution take on superhuman proportions in their capacity to evoke an unconditional loyalty and to have so profound an effect on a person's being that even in the rejection of Communism as a false god there remains a strange mixture of awe, guilt and regret. The role of Communism as a quasi-religion is especially evident in the experience of Silone; he knew what it meant to participate in the faith of one of the religions proper and, curiously enough, this made it both easier and harder for him to exchange allegiances. Easier, because in Catholicism he already understood the meaning of absolute authority in the Church, of revealed doctrines and a Pope who, on occasions, is said to wear the mantle of infallibility.[21] Silone could find counterparts in Communism for all this authority. Harder, because as one brought up within the Christian fold, he knew the meaning of idolatry, the paying homage to false gods, a fact that makes the title of the book especially poignant in his case.

The experience of Richard Wright who was born of poor Black parents in Mississippi in 1908 brings a new dimension into the Communist picture; unlike Koestler and Silone, Wright was born a member of the disinherited, and this had a profound effect on his decision to join the Communist Party through the John Reed Club in Chicago. As he points out, he was stirred in his initial reading of the *Masses* not by the economics of Communism, not by the working of trade unions, and not even by the lure of underground politics; 'my attention', he writes, 'was caught by the similarity of the experiences of workers in other lands, by the possibility of uniting scattered but kindred peoples into a whole' (p. 118). And he goes on to express what was closest to his heart – 'It seemed to me that here at last, in the realm of revolutionary expression, Negro experience could find a home, a functioning value and role' (ibid.). Wright, however, was no uncritical follower; he regarded what he read in Communist magazines as oversimplified in its treatment of the lives, experiences and passions of those whom it would lead. Here, as a writer, he saw a task for himself – 'I would tell Communists how common people felt, and I would tell common people of the self-sacrifice of Communists who strove for unity among them' (p. 120). Even more, Wright set out to make black people aware of the aims of Communism and he projected a series of biographical sketches of Negro Communists at the same time he confessed to himself 'how fantastically naive my ambition was' (p. 121).[22]

A crisis arose for him when he was told that the Party had made a decision that he was the one to organise a committee whose aim would be to bring the new message – 'defeat the Fascists' – to church people, club people, professionals, students and the middle class. Wright was uneasy in the face of this assignment and his reflection about it reveals once again the powerful hold the Party had upon its members. He knew, as he says, that a decision was 'the highest injunction that a Communist could receive from his Party' (p. 145) and that to break it meant breaking the Party's ability to act with a unified front. Wright believed this because he had come to his own conclusion that the oppressed can achieve political power only when they are united, and he had also come to believe that the Communist method of unity had shown itself to be 'the only means of achieving discipline' (ibid.). The fact is that he did not want to take on the assignment – he wanted to organise black artists in Chicago but was told that the Party did not need that now – yet he knew that refusal would mean that he was not a Communist after all.

We need not follow all the details, but it is clear that Wright wanted to retain some autonomy and when he asked that his name be dropped from the Party rolls, he was accused of being a Trotskyite and branded as a traitor. 'The Communist Party', Wright says, 'felt that it had to assassinate me morally merely because I did not want to be bound by its decisions' (p. 149). Wright's commitment to Communism came to an end in a humiliating and violent way. Although he wanted to march in the May Day parade of 1936 and had been invited to do so by a black Party member, he was physically prevented from joining the ranks – 'Hands lifted me bodily from the sidewalk; I felt myself being pitched headlong through the air' – and the worst of it was that he had 'suffered a public physical assault by two white Communists with black Communists looking on' (ibid.). It is clear that Wright's disillusionment was born of his perception that the Party placed its own priorities higher than the interests of any constituent group and, paradoxically enough, was unable to understand the plight of black people who, according to Marx's description of the revolutionary class, well qualified as those against which infinite crimes had been committed. Wright thus experienced in an especially cruel and demeaning way the consequences of idolatry, the elevating of a finite, fallible and fanatical Party to an absolute status. It would be more accurate to say that, for him, it was the *idol* that failed; the hallmark of a quasi-religion.

Although he was never a Party member, André Gide has expressed his great interest in what he regarded as the Communist experiment in Russia. 'It is not Marx', he wrote, 'who brought me to Communism . . . What brought me to Communism with my whole heart was the fact of the privileged position which I personally enjoy' (p. 170). He could not, he goes on to explain, continue to enjoy a comfortable life when so many around him were in want. In 1932 some fifteen years before a trip to Russia disillusioned him, Gide wrote in his *Journal* of his attraction to Communism and it is noteworthy that he described it in terms taken from religion:

My conversion is like a faith. My whole being is bent towards one
single goal, all my thoughts – even involuntary – lead me back
to it. In the deplorable state of distress of the modern world,
the plan of the Soviet Union seems to me to point to salvation.
(p. 173)

There is 'conversion' or the turn to the new truth that he calls a
'faith'. There is the sense of the commitment of his 'whole being'
which is reminiscent of the biblical injunction to love God with all
one's heart and soul and mind – the basis of Tillich's concept of
'ultimate concern'. There is, finally, the belief that the programme
of the Soviet Union points in the direction of 'salvation'. In the light
of Gide's religious background, it seems clear that he transferred
his allegiance from the Gospels to Communism and, like so many
others who have found a quasi-religion, it was accompanied by the
belief that Christianity had failed. His new faith, however, was not
to be sustained in the face of what he encountered during his visit
to Russia. The problem, again, has mainly to do with the tactics of
the Party. Although he believed at first in the show of self-criticism
which was standard practice, he soon discovered that it is not the
Party line that is to be criticised, but only whether some theory is or
is not in accord with that line. This he regarded as a 'dangerous'
state of mind and one that imperils all real culture.

Gide found that there were more disillusionments yet to come.
Instead of the Dictatorship of the Proletariat he found a 'dictatorship of the Soviet bureaucracy' (p. 184) in which, as he says, 'The
workers are cheated, muzzled and bound hand and foot, so that
resistance has become well-nigh impossible' (p. 185). He encountered
what he calls the depth of 'moral cynicism' when he learned that in
the model town of Bolchevo only those who had been informers
and betrayed others to the authorities were allowed to live there. In
response to his experiences, Gide decided that his task was to bring
the truth about the situation he found in Russia to Communists in
other parts of the world, but especially to the French Communist
Party; 'It is time', he writes, 'that the workers outside the Soviet
Union should realize that they have been bamboozled and led
astray by the Communist Party . . .' (p. 195). Gide saw the Party as
a power that declared itself to be absolute and not subject to the
demands of truth; the parallel here with Koestler's experience is
quite exact if we recall what he said about not having any longer to
bother with facts as soon as he learned the technique of 'dialectic'.

The experience of Louis Fischer, another contributor to *The God That Failed*, strikes many of the notes already sounded by his colleagues. An American journalist, Fischer was sent to Berlin in 1921 as correspondent for the *New York Post*. Like Gide, he was initially attracted to Communism as an experiment 'in the interest of the downtrodden' that might prove successful in upholding the cause of the common man and in providing land, food, a job, security – in short, the basic needs for a decent life. Fischer was fascinated by the Communist Party in Russia and described the basis of its appeal. 'In the requirements of austerity and dedication imposed on members', he wrote,

> it resembled a monastic order. Its tradition of automatic obedience, secrecy, and strict discipline made it kin to a military caste. It served as dynamo, watch dog, and inspiration of the regime. (p. 201)

In declaring himself a 'partisan' of the Soviet Union, Fischer offered an interesting rationale for his choice. General alignment with a cause, he says, transcends 'all but the most shocking facts about it' and he goes on to make a comparison with religious conviction and nationalism. The former is said to be impervious to logical argument and the latter can defy 'a mountain of evidence'. Similarly, Fischer confesses that in his attachment to the Soviet Union he regarded developments detrimental to Russia as merely ephemeral, or dishonestly interpreted and destined to be cancelled out by countervailing developments. There was, however, an incident, now well-known as the 'Kronstadt blood bath', when Soviet authorities ruthlessly crushed a sailors' revolt on the Island of Kronstadt, demonstrating thus their inhumane policy in the treatment of all political prisoners. This event led to public protest and sent shock waves to a number of prominent Party members. 'I had no "Kronstadt" for many years' Fischer writes, but he knew that such an event would have to happen in the course of Soviet affairs if he were ever to come to the point not merely of wavering or doubting but of openly attacking the cause. Such is the faith of converts.

As things turned out, Fischer's 'Kronstadt' came in August of 1939 in the form of the Soviet–Nazi Pact. He saw at once that the agreement was made to gain territory through a division of 'spheres of influence' between Germany and Russia which meant the beginning of Soviet planned aggression, with Stalin as the

'Supreme Slave Master'. Fischer's analysis of the 'timing' of a 'Kronstadt' in the experience of both Party members and sympathisers is very perceptive. The question is, What event is so objectionable that it will lead a person to 'leave the train'? Fischer's event was the Pact with the Nazis, but others managed to explain that away and did not abandon the cause until Russia invaded Finland in 1939. Even that was not the end for a 'well-known British radical' who did not find his 'Kronstadt' until Russia invaded Norway in 1940. This timing, Fischer says, depends on a number of temperamental factors; some were able to remain in the cause no matter what because of their belief that Socialist countries are incapable of 'sin', others were so obsessed by the crimes of capitalist countries that they blinded themselves to the crimes committed by the Bolsheviks, and harped on the defects of the West in order to divert attention from the horrors taking place in Russia. In the end, Fischer decided, as a 'free spirit' to turn his back on the evils of both worlds and strive instead for the creation of conditions in which 'dictatorships on both sides of the Iron Curtain would suffocate and perish' (p. 223).

Fischer's experience furnishes further evidence of the fatal flaw that ultimately vitiates every quasi-religion: the absolutising of some finite and conditioned reality – power, a political party, a nation, human beings, history, morality, etc. – so that it comes to stand beyond all critical judgement and, paradoxically enough, serves as a sanction for the same belief that 'all things are permitted' which was said to be the consequence of the 'death of God' declared by Nietzsche and celebrated by some latter-day theologians. And, indeed, it is precisely the rejection of God that opens the way for elevating some idol to divine status. As Fischer points out, one of Communism's central absolutes, in addition to that of the Party itself, was the supposedly moral principle that 'the end justifies the means' and its application in dictatorship which rests upon 'a sea of blood, an ocean of tears and a world of suffering'. Absolutes resist criticism and claim all for themselves; a hallmark of quasi-religions is that they fit this pattern and recognise no judgement from beyond. Consider by contrast the self-criticism to be found both in Judaism and in the Christianity of the Reformation. The Hebrew prophets from Amos to Isaiah attacked idolatry and false gods in the name of the true God made manifest to Moses, and Luther, in setting the Reformation on its course, declared that the Church, though the dispenser of judgement, is itself a *finite* reality which must see itself as also standing under the judgement of God. A touchstone for distinguishing quasi-religions from the religions proper is the extent to which the former acknowledge a principle of self-criticism sitting in judgement on their own absolutes.

Stephen Spender, the writer and poet, is the final contributor to *The God that Failed* and his experience does much to confirm what the other contributors had written. His case is singular in that he was a member of the British Communist Party for only a few weeks; he had paid his initial dues but was never invited to a meeting and, as he says, 'My membership lapsed soon after I had joined' (p. 229). He clearly had humanitarian leanings – 'What had impressed me most in the gospels was that all men are equal in the eyes of God, and that the riches of the few are an injustice to the many.' – and, like others, he believed that the Communist movement was aiming in the same direction. Early on, and not altogether to his liking, Spender encountered the power of the Marxist belief in 'history' and what was meant by being 'on the side of history' – the Dictatorship of the Proletariat and the establishment of Communism. Regardless of the cruelties which 'history' produced, it was essential to be on its side especially since it has no place for anyone not in the stream. In Spender's view, this faith in history was totally confined to the *future* which meant that one was free to disregard unpleasant realities such as the Moscow trials in the present, but also that no means were outlawed in the struggle to bring this future about. Spender was acutely aware of the tension between present and future as it was played out within his own mind. One can maintain faith in the future realisation of the goals of humanity, while ignoring the plight of those presently in prison camps or in compounds of slave workers, simply by regarding those being sacrificed as a necessary contribution to a good cause. As if debating with himself, Spender writes: 'The point is to fix one's eyes on the goal, and then one is freed of the horror and anxiety – quite useless in any case – which inhibit the energies of the liberal mind' (p. 238). He used to tell himself in an effort to strengthen his belief in the Communist cause, that with the triumph of the revolution the number of victims will decrease, for Communism does not need exploited people but only the 'cooperation of all men to make a better world' (ibid.).

We have witnessed similar attempts at self-persuasion in the experiences of Koestler, Silone and the others, but Spender appears to have had a particularly difficult time in trying to exorcise his 'liberal' conscience. 'For the intellectual of good will', he writes, 'Communism is a struggle of conscience', and he confesses that he found something overpowering in the 'fixed conscience' that is anchored in Marxist materialism (p. 240). 'A conscience', he continues, 'which tells us that by taking up a certain political position today we can attain a massive, granite-like superiority over our own whole past, without being humble or simple or guilty, but simply by converting the whole of our personality into raw material for the use of the Party machine!' (p. 241). In the end, Spender could not accept such a conscience and, with the shocking role played by the Communists in the Spanish Civil War vividly before him, he set about preparing to 'leave the train'. What troubled him most was what he saw as the encouragement by Communism of the human vice of self-righteousness where people regard their cause as the only reality and all other causes are merely 'outmoded theoretical positions'. The belief that the Communist cause is completely identifiable with the welfare of humanity and the inexorable course of history so that everyone else has either to be refuted or absorbed is a monstrous show of self-righteousness which, as Spender remarks, results in the dehumanisation of the Communists themselves. Nothing other than a dehumanised society can be the outcome of acting on principles that rob people of their humanity. Spender sums up this belief in a sentence: 'Communism is the belief that society can be altered by turning men into machines for altering society' (p. 271).

Although those whose experiences we have been considering came from different countries and had diverse backgrounds – social, economic, political – their involvement with Marxism, both their initial attraction to it and their ultimate rejection, shows that they shared certain features of personal character and philosophical outlook all of which throw light on the quasi-religious character of Communism. They all had moral and, in some cases, religious convictions of their own before they had anything to do with Marxism; they cared for human beings and were concerned about the unhappy lot of those who in one form or other were the victims of poverty, oppression and injustice wherever they lived. They were sensitive to the extent of their individual experience to the defects of the Western capitalist nations which, to be sure, had their own share of poverty, exploitation and, most prominent in the country of Richard Wright, racism. They also sensed that in these countries the moral principles derived from the Judeo-Christian tradition and from Enlightenment humanitarianism were eroding in the face of competitiveness, greed, the quest for money and power, and a 'survival of the fittest' mentality. They were experiencing doubts about the liberal political beliefs they shared because these beliefs – in human equality, civil rights, justice, peace – seemed no longer to have in the world of Ramsey MacDonald and Calvin Coolidge the reforming force they once had, for example, in Britain at the time of John Stuart Mill. It is important to remember that at the time this group was being attracted to Communism they had all the deficiencies of the West before them and did not yet know what was actually happening in Russia which they then regarded largely as a great 'experiment'. It was not difficult under those circumstances to throw one's lot in with the Communist 'experiment' in the hope that it would prove successful whereas it seemed to them that Western systems had already failed.

This group became fascinated by the Marxist vision of a new society on a global basis in which poverty, human exploitation and injustice would be overcome and the disinherited would find the conditions for decent living. The international or supra-national character of the movement had a special appeal; it was the common man in all countries who was to be redeemed, and it was hoped that a world-wide attack upon human ills would serve to decrease the evils of aggressive nationalism.

What, then, were the principal factors that led this group to confess that their new faith had failed? At the head of the list must come their ultimate refusal to countenance the tyranny and tactics of the Party. Rigorous discipline and the call for sacrifice may have an initial appeal – as it no doubt did – but the discovery that those who preached freedom as over against the slavery of capitalist systems, and truth as opposed to bourgeois lies, had no regard for either freedom or truth, was too much to swallow. These were highly intelligent men with much knowledge and experience; they were prepared to argue in a rational way and they demanded straightforward answers, but what they received instead were commands to obey without question the Party line, even when it turned at a moment's notice into the opposite of what it was before, and to learn how either to ignore patent facts or to explain them away with the help of Marxist dialectic. Perhaps even more alienating than the demand that they sacrifice their intelligence was the affront to their moral sensibility represented by the ruthless application of the end justifying the means principle. They understood

how readily the adherents of a cause can convince themselves that
a concern for whether a given means to the end is 'good' or not is
irrelevant, a carry-over of the 'liberal' conscience, since a good
cause cannot have 'bad' means. They understood as well the two
features of the Communist mentality which both intensifies and
confirms this belief; if one has the only 'right' cause and all others
are worthless, assessment of the human or moral quality of means
fades into the background, and if one has the cause that is destined
to be realised or has 'history' on its side, the end becomes so
absolute a priority that in its service 'all is permitted'. The experience and insight of these thinkers, moreover, taught them that no
human socio-political order can result from tactics involving the
ruthless manipulation of people, lying and informing, the purging
of dissidents and other means of terror. Only a fool will believe that
political means are the same as hammers and shovels which can be
set aside once their functions have been performed.

Not least among the reasons why these converts and sympathisers finally decided to abandon the cause was to be found in plain
historical reality – the terrible contrast between Communist ideals
and claims and the actual living conditions of those who were
supposed to benefit most from the new society. This betrayal, dis-
guised as far as possible by propaganda or openly 'justified' as
sacrifices required in the 'meantime' for the future success of the
revolution, opened their eyes to the failure of the Communist movement, the hollowness of their newly found faith. And in fairness to
Marx's vision at its best, it seems clear enough that he would have
regarded the Russian 'experiment' as nothing less than a travesty of
his own prophetic diagnosis of the human predicament and his
revolutionary solution. That Marxism, however, could enlist the
devotion and the faith, as they put it, of the Koestlers, the Gides, the
Wrights and the others testifies amply to its power as a quasi-
religion. As they expressed it, joining the cause in whatever capacity was something far more momentous than joining a political
party or a society; it meant enlisting their whole being in a movement that had history on its side and was destined to overcome the
ills of man and society. The apocalyptic fervor was unmistakable
and this made the final downfall all the more catastrophic. After all,
this was no ordinary disillusionment; it was the 'God' that failed.

For those who experienced it directly, the awesome contrast between the actual living conditions prevailing in Russia at the time
and the professed Communist ideals, raised insurmountable doubts.

These, moreover, were intensified by the Soviet propaganda aimed at concealing these conditions from the rest of the world, not to mention from the Soviet peoples themselves. In addition, the reign of terror initiated by Stalin was utterly repugnant to these individuals no one of whom could advocate violence.

The role of the Communists in the Spanish Civil War was another major stumbling-block that could neither be justified nor explained away through any dialectic. Part of the initial attraction of Communism for these intellectuals was its claim to overcome aggressive nationalism through a truly international movement, aimed at liberating the oppressed throughout the world, but again this hope was sadly disappointed by both the Spanish War and the totalitarian regime in Russia. Finally, Koestler and his colleagues ceased to believe in the *necessity* of the historical process as preached by the prophets of world revolution and, in fact, the Communists themselves came to have their own doubts on this head as can be seen in the disappearance of references to the 'iron laws of history' which was one of Marx's favourite phrases.

The break-up of the Soviet Union and the painful reshaping of Eastern Europe which is now taking place must be the material of future historians and in any case it is not a matter relevant for our present purposes. There is, however, a fundamental aspect of the situation which is of importance and it allows us to make a comparison between the plight of Communist intellectuals in the years prior to the rise of Gorbachev and the experiences of those intellectuals who were attracted by Communism more than a half-century ago. The Soviet journalist, Len Karpinsky, has described the dilemmas faced by the intellectuals of recent years. 'So many people', he writes, 'have been destroyed',

> You can maintain that split way of thinking for a while, but when you begin to degenerate and start to speak only what is permitted, and the rest of the conscience and the soul decays. Many people did not survive to *perestroika*. We had to create an internal moral system, and not everyone could sustain that indefinitely . . . we tried not to live by lies, but we couldn't always manage it.[23]

Here we have confirmation from the inside, as it were, of the same split consciousness that finally erodes the person which the authors of *The God that Failed* experienced and which finally led them to 'leave the train' – the train of a quasi-religion.

4

Nationalism as a Quasi-Religion

In comparison with Humanism and Marxism, Nationalism is by far the more complex phenomenon to encompass. The American historian, Carlton J. H. Hayes, a pioneer in the study of nationalism, called attention decades ago to the enormous problems facing any scholar attempting to analyse and appraise the phenomenon of patriotism and national sentiment to be found in every country throughout the world. In Hayes's view, nationalism expresses not only the aspirations – political, ethnic, cultural, religious – of a people, but it evokes and lives from deep-seated and powerful emotions, so that to understand nationalism demands, in addition to a knowledge of history and the history of ideas, philosophy, social psychology, anthropology and linguistics.[1] It is, however, not only the vast scope of the topic and the countless forms nationalism has assumed that is troublesome at the outset; there is the more subtle problem of finding a way to draw the line between what we may call the legitimate and 'natural' patriotism through which people affirm and take pride in having a national identity – 'this is my own, my native land', says the poet – and the modern phenomenon of an 'artificial' nationalism which stems from an ideal conception of a nation – its having a 'mission' in world history, for example – which is re-enforced through education and propaganda aimed at engaging the loyalty of great masses of people.[2] There is something of value in a clear-headed and heart-felt patriotism which expresses an individual's affirmation of belonging to a people taken in the sense in which it is commonplace to speak of the French, English, German or American people. Nationalism, however, goes far beyond this natural bond of belonging to a people; it involves making special claims for a nation, its power and prestige, and often means tyrannising the inhabitants of a nation in the pursuit of chauvinistic aims which pose a constant threat to world peace. Since it is nationalism which we are considering as a quasi-religion of its own – it will be helpful for a beginning to try to describe what I have called

the 'natural' patriotism or sense of pride in belonging to a people
and having a *patria* or homeland which at the very least enables a
person to distinguish between being at 'home' and being 'abroad'.[3]
The important point is that this natural sense of belonging and
having a national identity of some sort is essential to all civilised
life and it must not be confused with nationalism which is essentially a redirection of this natural bond between human beings. The
intricacy of the situation becomes clear when we consider that all
forms of nationalism seek to establish their hold on a people by
appealing to, and even by trying to incorporate within itself, this
natural bond of patriotism. In his classic essay, 'What is Nationalism?', Hayes points out that nationalism is a fusion of patriotism
and what he calls 'nationality' or the extension of patriotism as a
local loyalty to a *national* state or even to an empire.

Despite the fact that Hayes's studies in nationalism predate the
appearance of the nationalism embodied in Nazi Germany, the
Italy of Fascism, the imperialism of Japan and the 'mission' to
extend Democracy in latter-day American nationalism, there is still
much to be learned from his astute analysis of the nature of the
realities we envision in such terms as 'nation', 'nationality', 'nationalism', and 'patriotism'.

To begin with, the term 'nation', according to Hayes, is the most
ambiguous of the lot, having sustained a variety of meanings over
the centuries. The term has been used to designate groupings based
on birth, race and a real or only supposed community of language;
physicians and lawyers have been described as 'nations', and since
the seventeenth century it has been customary to think of a nation
as a sovereign political authority without regard to racial or lin-
guistic unity among the populace. Earlier on, in the universities of
the Middle Ages student groups or guilds were known as 'nations'
based on their place of birth and used to determine voting rights so
that in the French universities of the time, for example, students
from other countries such as Germany and Scotland made up
'nations' and French students belonged to 'nations' which were
identified through regions – Lorraine, Burgundy, Champagne, etc.[4]
And in America the term came to stand for the American people as
a whole represented by the federal government as distinct from the
governments of the individual states.

If the chief connotation of the term 'nation' was *political*, in the
early nineteenth century another term, 'nationality', came into use
and it expressed the *cultural* dimension of social groupings.

According to Hayes, this term is far less ambiguous than 'nation' and was used to designate 'a group of people who speak either the same language or closely related dialects, who cherish common historical traditions, who constitute or think they constitute a distinct cultural society'.[5] In these terms a nationality can exist without a sovereign state of its own, and a political state might be made up of several nationalities.

With these distinctions in hand it becomes possible to delineate more clearly the phenomenon of *nationalism* as an historical reality which came upon the scene in the nineteenth century when the word itself first came into use in the languages of Europe. Numerous scholars agree that the primary and most tangible feature of nationalism is the drive to organise existing nationalities into a political unity which is the modern national state. To carry out this process it was necessary, in addition, to have an ideal or principle which at one and the same time embraces a heightening of the sense of nationality and a political philosophy centring on the idea of the state. Thus, in the nature of the case, nationalism depends heavily on a rationale informing the consciousness of a people. Arieli has expressed the point very well; 'Nationalism', he writes,

> rises beyond the loyalties to ancient traditions or the attachment of men to their land, their home, and the localities to which they belong. It is founded upon generalizations and a conceptual framework of orientation – in short, upon ideology. (Arieli, p. 1)

One may not want to prejudge the case with the use of the term 'ideology', especially if it implies a tissue of self-deception or the deliberate masking of special interests behind professedly high ideals. Perhaps 'idealisation' would be a better word, since the philosophies expressed in nationalism inevitably appeal, not so much to a *de facto* political reality, as to ideals of what the state stands for and what it may *become*. Howsoever it may be characterised, it is clear that a political philosophy is necessary for nationalism to be established. To take but one example, Hegel's *Philosophy of Right*, or his theory of the modern national state, played a significant role in the unification of Germany in the nineteenth century and the discussion still goes on concerning its influence on the rise of National Socialism under Hitler.

Although nationalism as a rule aims at achieving unity in a national state, there are countless examples in modern and recent

history where a particular group, usually a political party representing a minority within a country as a whole, appropriates the
name of a 'Nationalist' party and seeks to unify its constituents by
appealing to their concern to protect their own identity in a situation where it is threatened by majority power. Instances abound;
one has only to point to such typical cases as Ireland and the force
of Irish national sentiment in the face of British rule; Muslim nationalism in the Punjab and the formation of Pakistan at the time of
India's gaining freedom from Britain in 1947; and the even more
striking case of South Africa where the African National Congress
struggled to gain political recognition for an overwhelming
majority of black people in a country ruled by a white minority.
These and many other instances must be counted as manifestations
of nationalism, but on a lesser scale than the nationalism represented by the unified, national state.

There remains yet another feature of nationalism – in many ways
the most important even if the least tangible – and that is the frame
of mind, the attitude, the loyalty and devotion of the people which
is the life force of all nationalisms. Since it is this feature of the topic
which will engage most of our attention in the sequel, I shall do no
more for the present than call attention to its significance. Hayes
has described this frame of mind in succinct terms; it is, he writes,
'a condition of mind in which loyalty to the ideal or to the fact of
one's national state is superior to all other loyalties and of which
pride in one's nationality and belief in its intrinsic excellence and in
its 'mission' are integral parts' (Hayes, p. 6). As we shall see, no
feature of nationalism has been more powerful in capturing the
imagination and the patriotic spirit of a people than the idea,
whether based on fact or fiction, that the country has some 'mission'
to be accomplished in world history, some special contribution to
make to human progress, some 'manifest destiny' to be fulfilled in
the course of events. This belief in the existence of a national aim or
purpose is intensified when it is accompanied by a sense that the
country has been 'called' – whether by God, progress, or the historical process itself in the form of 'the wave of the future' – to carry
out an appointed task for which it is uniquely equipped. So strong
has this sense been that dictators in totalitarian regimes have often
spoken as though they were instruments of a higher power and
were ordained to carry out their mission even against their own will.
Hans Kohn has described this feature of nationalism in a succinct
way: 'in the age of nationalism some nations have proclaimed for

themselves a "mission" here on earth: the divine right of kings was replaced by the divine right of nations. Messianic dreams with the nation at their center put the nation into immediate and independent relations with the Absolute' (Kohn, p. 8). Although examples abound, Kohn cites the particularly striking case of India at the end of the last century. In 1885, with the help of English liberals, the Indian National Congress was formed and with it the discovery of India's unique task on the world scene, 'A mission', Kohn writes, 'was discovered for India: Indian religious spiritualism and metaphysical profundity were to save Europe from Western materialism, a craving for physical (superficial) comfort, and competitive strife' (Kohn, p. 6). Echoes of this mission can still be heard more than a century later. I have attended numerous international conferences of philosophers and religious thinkers over the past 25 years and many Indian philosophers still believe very much in this mission, the only change being that 'America' would be added to the list of countries needing salvation.

Since there is general agreement among those who have studied nationalism in some depth that it is a cultural phenomenon, a work of art and artifice which goes beyond local loyalties in appealing to aims and interests of a national state, it will be helpful to consider some of the proposals which have been made to explain the basis of nationality and patriotism regarded as the 'natural' loyalties upon which nationalism must establish itself.[6] Nationalism, in short, will stand out more clearly as the result of setting it apart from these lesser bonds that serve to unify peoples and define the nationalities of which modern states are composed.

I am indebted in what follows to the clear and well illustrated analyses of Hayes in his efforts to find the essential bases for the identification of nationalities. I believe, however, that one rider should be attached to his account and it is that while the features he cites – geography, race etc. – all fall short as forming *the* basis of nationality, there can be no question that each plays some essential role in constituting national identities. As one might expect, given the enormous variety of conditions throughout the countries of the world, some one feature, whether language, human gregariousness, the 'national mind' and others, will figure more prominently in one situation than in another.

Hayes is surely correct in rejecting the idea that the human tendency to live and work in groups forms the basis of nationality, for it is obvious that there are groups that share common concerns –

religious, economic, educational, etc. – which are by no means limited to this or that nation, but are international in scope. He is also on sound ground in questioning the belief that geography is the maker of nationalities; there are too many instances to the contrary. Even if, as Hayes notes, the fact that islands like Britain and Japan are separated from large continents, and America consists of a large part of a continent far distant from Europe and Asia has certainly played some part in the formation of their nationalities, there is much that cannot be explained in this way. The British Isles contain four or more nationalities; the Iberian Peninsula has within it Portuguese, Castillian, Catalan, and Basque nationalities; the Greek nationality is distributed over many a rock and many an isle. Hayes concludes that 'the idea of natural frontiers between nationalities is a myth' (p. 7).

Equally suspect on Hayes's list of candidates supposed to provide the basis of nationality is the idea of race. To begin with, the very notion of race is itself a muddle, and even if it were not there is no getting around the fact that all modern nationalities are racial mixtures and that there exists no such thing as 'racial purity'. In discussing the matter, Hayes makes a side comment that is nothing short of prophetic when viewed in the light of the Holocaust that occurred in this century. While insisting that nationality cuts both through and across race, 'it must be confessed', he writes, 'in deference to racial propaganda, that an imaginary belief in blood relationship, that is, in race, has been an effective force in building and cementing nationalities' (p. 8). Nazism appealed to just such an 'imaginary belief' in its claims about a 'pure Aryan' race and combined it with the symbols of blood and soil in order to command the loyalty of a vast majority of the German people, except that Hitler's programme went far beyond mere nationalism and extended to the horrors of the 'final solution' aimed at exterminating the Jewish people and any others guilty of defiling the 'purity' of the Aryan people. What is most insidious about this sort of emphasis on race is that the idea of a 'pure' race calls up images of a noble past from which it is supposed to stem and also establishes as targets of hatred all those who are believed to be polluting it. The tragic fact is that the resort to race as a rallying cry for national identity must, in the nature of the case, be an appeal to what is basically false. And this remains so even if nationalities have not been noted for any great concern about the truth of their national self-portraits.

Hayes's prophetic statement about nationalism based on an appeal to blood relationship still continues to be validated by recent history. No more striking case can be found than the shocking and tragic events that have been taking place since the summer and fall of 1991 in the break-up of the Yugoslavian federation, a development which came on the heels of a similar, but far more extensive, breakup of the Soviet Union. The bloody struggles involving Serbs, Croats, Slovenes and the Muslim populations of Bosnia and Kosovo together with the 'ethnic cleansing' that is taking place demonstrate the fanatic proportions to which nationalism based on racial 'purity' can mount. Serbia, the largest and wealthiest republic, saw a new opportunity to enlarge itself even further under the familiar banner of 'a greater Serbia', while Croatia and Slovenia followed suit in their quest for independence. In addition to these conflicts of national interest there are religious divisions going back for centuries; the Croats and Slovenes are Roman Catholics; the Serbs belong to the Eastern Orthodox Church, while Bosnia-Herzogovina and Kosova are largely Muslim and a living reminder, especially to the Serbs and Croats, of the centuries of oppression they endured under the Ottoman Empire. Although no one can discount the force of these religious differences, the nationalism of Serbia especially is racially oriented which accounts for the zeal with which they have engaged in the massacre of Muslims.

The truly demonic nature of a nationalism appealing to belief in racial purity is manifest in its utter finality; such nationalism must end with *genocide*, since it is motivated by a concern far deeper than animosities stemming from differences in language, customs, economic power, etc. The goal is nothing less than the elimination of an 'impure' enemy. To highlight the profound difference involved, we have only to consider, for example, the tensions existing in Canada between English speaking and French speaking Canadians. These tensions, though real enough, are nothing in comparison with what we have been witnessing recently in Bosnia, Somalia and Kurdistan. The great desire of the French Canadians to have their own national identity and culture certainly does not include doing away with those they oppose.

Nationalities do indeed differ from each other in following distinctive social customs as can be seen from the associations that come readily to mind when we think of food, drink, clothing, sports and social practices in countries throughout the world. The English drink tea and the Germans drink beer; Italians love garlic and, like the French, wine; the peoples of India relish curry and a spicy cuisine; the women in Muslim countries must be veiled; Americans have baseball as a national game, while in Australia cricket and tennis hold the spotlight; in most countries of Europe and in many countries in Latin America soccer holds sway. There is certainly a measure of national identity to be found in such characteristic customs as there is also in what has been called a 'national mind'. The ideals and guiding principles of a nation extend beyond the confines of individual minds and cannot be understood as the 'sum' – whatever that means in this context – of what individuals believe. Ideas, as Charles Peirce was fond of saying, *spread* throughout a culture and have their own way of both expressing and evoking some community of thought and action. Bastille Day in France, for example, and the 4th of July in America have assumed the force of national symbols whose principal meaning is well known to all the inhabitants of both countries regardless of what any single individual or even group of individuals may think about the matter. What is frequently overlooked, however, is that national minds and their partners, national characters – that the French think clearly, that the Germans have discipline, that the English are the champions of political liberty etc. – are by no means constant. How could one imagine Imperial Japan with its long history of isolation and fear of the outside world ever becoming as it is today an advanced industrial nation with interests and ties all over the world. In another vein, earlier generations of Americans had a sober sense of what sacrifices might be needed in order to maintain a political order in which life, liberty and the pursuit of happiness were viable ideals. But less than two decades ago, President Jimmy Carter met with a huge rebuke by many segments of the population when he dared to suggest that sacrifices might be needed on the part of all in order to resolve the problems that plague American society – poverty, racism, homelessness, the spread of violence and mindless crime, drug abuse and, unfortunately, many others.

Nationality, then, must be based on more constant and enduring foundations than any of those we have noted. To the extent to which a nationality endures, it must find its roots in a culture which means in the existence of a common language, in an allegiance to common historical traditions and in a self-consciousness that acknowledges these common bonds. Patriotism is the natural form of such an acknowledgement and it has existed for as far back as we

are able to go in human history. But, as Hayes points out, patriotism manifests itself initially as a *local* affair as we can see, to take but
one example, from the history of ancient Greece, where it was
attached to the city-states of Athens, Sparta, Corinth and not to all
Greek speaking people. The point is most important because the
development of nationalism out of nationality and patriotism requires the extension of both forms from a native locality, first, to a
political country, and then to a political or military leader, ending
with the idea of the national *state*.[7] It is the need for this extension
of loyalty beyond its local habitat which leads Hayes and others to
describe the imperial patriotism that issues in nationalism as 'artificial' because it is dependent on inherited social knowledge and
requires a conscious effort beyond what is necessary for local
patriotism.

Nationalism as we now know it began as a phenomenon in the
modern world because the idea of a national state also made its
appearance in this same world. The first problem facing those who
would foster nationalism in a state concerns the transfer of the
loyalty and patriotism people feel for local and visible communities
to the national and far less visible state. For such people the
national state is, quite literally, a 'city out of sight' and to evoke the
sentiment of nationalism among them necessarily requires a con-
certed and self-conscious effort. We see this well illustrated in
America with its three focal units – local communities, the individual states and the nation as a whole. Except in times of war and
in cases of international conflicts of interest, the nation is the least
visible reality, while the local community retains its most vivid
presence and the states fall somewhere in between the two. It was
with this in mind and to compensate for the impersonality and
invisibility of the nation, that years ago John Dewey, harking back
to Jefferson's idea of the town meeting – the 'face to face' community – called for an extension of this type of community forum
as a means whereby people could regain some sense of participation in the affairs of their country. The underlying problem is, of
course, that of the *size* of a nation and the effect it has on the
relations between individuals, communication, loyalty and indeed
the entire fabric of social life.

It is interesting to note how great a role was played by the factor
of *size* as regards both territory and population in political thinking about the state. Some thinkers perceived that magnitude affects *quality* in every region of experience, including the political.

A seminar of a dozen students has an atmosphere of community and communication which does not exist in a lecture class of 300 students; the family with its intimacies, emotional ties, and unspoken rules of behaviour is no model for the organisation of a civil society. Plato thought that the maximum number of citizens in an ideal state could be no more than 5040 if patriotism were to be sustained. And Hegel, one of the philosophical architects of the modern national state, maintained that a government perfectly adequate for the needs of the limited size of a Swiss Canton would hardly be appropriate for the state a theory of whose foundations and organisation he set forth in *The Philosophy of Right*.

In the past century and a half, the situation has greatly changed; conditions of natural patriotism and home grown loyalty have given way to the nationalist creed. Hayes has summed up the change in a clear and pointed way. 'Nowadays', he writes, there is preached and practised.

> a two-fold doctrine, (1) that each nationality should constitute a united independent sovereign state, and (2) that every national state should expect and require of its citizens not only unquestioning obedience and supreme loyalty, not only an exclusive patriotism, but also unshakable faith in its surpassing excellence over all other nationalities and lofty pride in its peculiarities and its destiny. This is nationalism and it is a modern phenomenon. (p. 26)

Three ideas are of special importance in this formula; first, that nationalism is expressed in a doctrine that must be proclaimed much like a creed which is to say that it is a self-conscious doctrine to be believed by a people; second, that the independent sovereign state is the recognised unit of political organisation and the framework within which a culture exists; and third, that the state demands that it be not only the supreme loyalty in the lives of its citizens, but that this loyalty is to be directed not to the bare existence of the state itself, but to certain claims made by the state about its superiority to other states, its special qualities and its destiny, usually seen as some 'mission' it has to perform in the course of world history.

The development of nationalism in Europe and America in the past two centuries is of less relevance for our purpose than is an understanding of the fact that it is an outlook which must be propagated through a conscious effort to influence the minds and to engage the hearts of a people. Although the term 'propaganda' has taken on a largely pejorative meaning due to the evil forms it has assumed, we must not overlook a more neutral sense of the term in which it means forms of expression intended to communicate or spread a message. At its worst, propaganda can be the dissemination of lies, and at its best, it is a form of persuasion in behalf of the ideas that underlie a cause. Without, for the present at least, making judgements about the validity of nationalist causes, it is important to understand that, while nationalisms do indeed appeal to already existing native patriotisms, they go beyond those sentiments through a conscious effort to establish loyalty and obedience to a sovereign state. The point is re-enforced when we consider the pattern, illustrated many times over in the history of nationalism, through which the message of the nation is formed and communicated. There is first the need for a group of economists, philosophers, historians and, in the case of Germany in the nineteenth century, philologists and folklorists, whose task is to 'define' the country, its ideals, virtues, goals and destiny.[8] Second, this interpretation of the country must find support among the powerful and influential in the society, both individuals and groups, either through their willingness to espouse the country's aims in a patriotic spirit or their perception that it is in accord with their own interests to do so. Finally, it is necessary to instil the doctrine in the popular mind, usually, as Hegel pointed out, through a national leader who convinces the populace that their will is really the same as the national will which the leader represents. It is this process that writers about nationalism have in mind when they describe it as an 'artificial' phenomenon, an outlook and a loyalty sustained by artifice.

As an introduction to interpreting the phenomenon of nationalism as a quasi-religion, we may consider the perceptive analysis offered by Hayes in which he goes even further and openly describes nationalism 'as a religion'. The obvious justification for making this identification is that nationalism, like the religions proper, offers a cause, an object for supreme loyalty and devotion and demands both sacrifice and obedience. It is, however, doubtful, even after allowing for the similarities which can be pointed out, that nationalism can fulfil all the functions of religion, or even that it can fulfil adequately those religious needs and aspirations which seem closest to being replaced by nationalistic programmes. Notwithstanding, Hayes has presented a case that is worthy of attention.

Citing the deep-seated human capacity for loyalty and the existence in all cultures of a 'religious sense'[9] expressing itself in all the forms of positive religion, Hayes puts a most pertinent question: 'Is it not a demonstrable fact', he writes, 'that nationalism has become to a vast number of persons a veritable religion, capable of arousing that deep and compelling emotion which is essentially religious?' (p.94). In the attempt to answer his own question, Hayes rightly points out how often in the past scepticism concerning a particular religion or even about the 'supernatural' itself has led to faith in a new form of religion. The situation in eighteenth-century Europe illustrates this development very well; attacks upon Christianity and all forms of superstition so-called, made in the name of reason, gave way to a religion of Nature and other forms of 'natural religion' and ultimately to faith in new gods – Progress, Perfectionism, Science, and Humanity. The French Revolution, moreover, gave birth to a nationalism that assumed religious proportions when The Declaration of the Rights of Man and of the Citizen was named the 'national catechism'.[10] That this is no exaggeration can be seen in the decree of the Legislative Assembly in 1792 that, 'in all the communes an altar to the Fatherland shall be raised, on which shall be engraved the Declaration of Rights . . .' (Hayes, p.103). The proclamation of devotion to *La Patrie* as a new 'lay religion' followed directly upon new waves of anti-clericalism and new attacks on Catholic Christianity; the impetus for the new religion was derived from the rejection of the old.

Largely because of his belief that the idea of the modern state is very close to the medieval notion of the Church, Hayes is quite sanguine in drawing up a list of parallels between Christianity and the new nationalism. The Fatherland assumes the place of a god upon which the individual feels dependent for his or her well-being and to which persons willingly subject themselves. The imagination that works in nationalism constructs an 'unseen world' encompassing an 'eternal past' and an unending future for the nation. Like the medieval church, the national state embodies an idea and a mission which Hayes envisages as a form of 'salvation' for all who serve the national cause. The individual is born into the national state, just as he or she was born into the Church and in both cases there is instruction, religious doctrine in the one and the articles of patriotism in the other.

Significant as these parallels are, deeper affinities make themselves felt in the sphere of ritual and symbolism. Hayes is quite right in pointing to the national flag as the supreme symbol of devotion; expression of faith in the nation is made in the 'salute' to the flag, and, indeed, one could go further and say that the flag itself becomes a *sacred* object guarded by strict regulations concerning when and how it is to be displayed – raised, lowered, folded, etc. – and by severe penalties for 'insults' to and 'desecration' of the official banner. The ultimate test of this loyalty can be seen in the national crises which resulted in America several years ago when protestors, acting in the name of the civil rights they thought synonymous with the American tradition, burned the flag in order to shock the nation into an awareness of how many of these rights were being violated. Similar illustrations can be found in such international athletic competitions as the Olympic Games where the National flag stands at the head of each nation's competitors and then follows the problem of whether a nation's flag can be 'lowered' before the flag of the host nation as a gesture of respect.[11] Considering the enormous spiritual power resident in the combination of words and music, it is not difficult to see how important national anthems are in expressing the nationalist spirit. 'Deutschland über Alles' says something more than the idea that loyalty to Germany should outweigh all other loyalties for the German citizen; the idea of supremacy among nations is even more forcefully expressed in 'Rule Britannia'. In a similar vein, the Austrian Hymn declares that 'glorious things of thee are spoken' and the object of such praise is nothing less than Zion, the city of God. It is in these situations that the contrast becomes most clear between a patriotism expressing love of one's country and an aggressive nationalism which demands superiority of the nation in the name of its perceived virtue over all other nations. Writing about the place of literature in the work of the composer Franz Liszt, Jacques Barzun makes an incisive comment about this contrast. 'To the Romanticists', he writes,

> the love of nation did not mean an aggressive self-satisfied attitude toward other peoples. On the contrary, it meant an appreciation of diversity among the national traditions. The nations of Europe were compared to a bouquet of cultures, each with its characteristic fragrance.[12]

There is no denying that the parallels between the symbols that give expression to the ideals and aspirations of nationalism and the symbols that give embodiment to the dominant religious faith of Western civilisation are both very close and, on that account, very striking. And these parallels assume even greater importance when a secular attitude gains in strength so that those who have come to regard many religious practices as mere 'superstition' have no hesitation in wrapping the mantle of the sacred around the national holidays of their country, their Founding Fathers and military heroes and their national shrines whether these be the birthplaces of these heroes or objects of veneration such as Britain's *Magna Carta* and America's Liberty Bell. The development is essentially a transposition of the sacred from the properly religious sphere to the cult of the nation.[13] The move, moreover, from sacred to secular is seductive in the extreme, since religious faith is a risk and a venture into what Gabriel Marcel has called the Mystery of Being, a commitment to things unseen and to a city out of sight, whereas participation in the national cult is based on what is there for all to see – the visible symbols of national pride and public consciousness. For most the transposition is easy to make, its costs are few and its rewards are many. This is not to say that one cannot retain a religious faith along with a love of one's country; it is rather that in times when a secular spirit prevails and religion finds itself subordinated to other interests, the cult of the nation presents itself as a virtually irresistible substitute, a quasi-religion all the more powerful since it has, so to speak, a built-in sanction. To be suspected of being unpatriotic or of calling into question the ideals and aspirations from which nationalism draws its strength are readily taken as defects of character if not as outright crimes. We see this happen most clearly in situations where different national interests come into conflict with each other; those favouring the use of military power to settle such disputes – generally named 'hawks' – represent themselves as the true 'patriots' in behalf of the country, while those who are less sanguine about the use of armed force and believe that mediation and negotiation should be tried – generally named 'doves' – are often branded as 'unpatriotic' and are often accused of disloyalty.[14] The situation in America in what has now come to be known as the 'McCarthy Era', provides an even more forceful illustration. The enemy was Communism and Communists, whether actual members of the Party or those who had merely attended, often a decade before, a meeting or a rally held under Communist auspices. The House Committee on unAmerican Activities inaugurated a 'witch hunt' in which individuals were black-listed – the members of the motion picture industry were a prime target – as traitors and in some cases imprisoned. So sanguine were these defenders of the nation and its honour that they did not hesitate to engage in the favourite tactic used by the Communist Party namely, threatening to expose as disloyal suspects who refused to betray their associates. All this was done in the name of patriotism, freedom and democracy and motivated by an irrational fear of Communism; what made these Congressional investigations even more abhorrent was the *inversion* of the principle basic to the American legal system that each individual is innocent until proven guilty by due process of law. Senator McCarthy and his henchmen flouted this principle under the aegis of sophistical argument that if a person is really innocent – in this case, is not a 'Communist' – he or she has nothing to fear in taking a Loyalty Oath. Those who rejected this specious argument rightly described it as 'Guilty by suspicion'. Nationalism is not free of the fanaticism that is generally supposed to be the exclusive property of religion.

In making his case for nationalism as a religion, Hayes cites even more parallels between nationalism and religion than I have mentioned. Every national state, he says, has a 'theology' in the form of doctrines derived from the 'Fathers' and woven into an official mythology which often subordinates objective truth to the demands of nationalist zeal.[15] And, like religious instruction in the churches, the public school system of the state is responsible for teaching this theology and for certifying that the curriculum accurately expresses the national faith. He also draws a striking comparison between the forms of intolerance to be found in modern states and the attitude of the Medieval Christian to unbelievers. Hayes's point is that the Christian was harsher to heretics than to infidels, pagans and Jews and he finds exact counterparts to these groups in modern national states; infidels and pagans at home, i.e., unnaturalised immigrants, are accepted, if they are few in number, in the hope that they will eventually 'fit in', but if their numbers are large and they seem reluctant to assimilate and accept the nation's creed, barriers are set up against them. Heretics are countrymen who have lapsed from the faith, either as outright traitors or as what Hayes calls 'crypto-heretics' – those who are indifferent to patriotic duties and are suspected of having a secret allegiance to another country. Included in this category would also be those who have the highest regard for the country's heritage but who criticise and protest such actions abroad and such legislation at home which they believe betray that heritage. Häns Kohn confirms Hayes's contention when he writes, 'Only a very few centuries ago, Man's loyalty was due to his church or his religion, a heretic put himself beyond the pale of society as a "traitor" to his nation does today.'[16]

Despite all these parallels between nationalism and Christianity, Hayes knows that in the end nationalism falls far short of the resources to be found in the religions proper and he offers a few reasons for his conclusion. I shall mention them as a prelude to further discussion attempting to show why nationalism at best (or worst) can be no more than a quasi-religion or the turning of what is finite and conditioned – the national state – into an object of *absolute* value which nothing transcends. Hayes levels three charges against nationalism; in contrast to the *unifying* force exercised chiefly by Buddhism, Islam[17] and Christianity, nationalism has proved to be a *disintegrating* factor since it is based ultimately on a *tribal* idea, or, as Hayes puts it, 'The good at which [nationalism] aims is a good for one's own nation only, not for all mankind'.[18] Secondly, nationalism leads to the proliferation of 'chosen peoples' and this poses a constant threat to world peace. Finally, and most important, nationalism is concerned neither with charity nor justice, but is proud and runs directly counter to the Christian idea that there shall be neither Jew nor Greek but one mankind. There will still be, to be sure, Jew and Greek but their being as human persons must transcend both their national and ethnic identity.

Hayes has indeed pointed out some grave defects in nationalism, defects which serve to show that it cannot take a place side by side with the religions proper. There are, however, other and perhaps deeper reasons why this is so and why nationalism must be regarded instead as a quasi-religion, for, as I shall suggest, even if nationalism has some of the ingredients of a religion, it does not have all of them and what it lacks are the most important. Like religion, nationalism provides a cause or an object of loyalty and dedication, a cause for which people will make sacrifices, even of their life if need be in the case of war, international crises involving terrorism, the taking of hostages, etc. The fact is, however, that people tend to be willing to sacrifice for the nation only when its life or its 'honour' are threatened, which means, of course, their own life or way of living. In time of peace when the threat of war which is the most powerful force uniting a nation is lacking, the motivation to sacrifice for the good of the nation in other ways virtually disappears. It is not by accident that when a government wants to enlist the support of the people in dealing with urgent internal problems – poverty, crime, drug abuse – it declares a 'war' on these evils in the hope of evoking that same unity of resolve which shows itself when the nation is involved in an armed conflict with another nation or nations.

Nationalism can provide a focus for unifying the self, for presenting a cause in which one can literally *find* oneself through its service, but this is true only to a limited extent. It has not often been recognised that a total self-fulfilment in one kind of service to the nation is to be found only in the professional military class, or perhaps also in the case of the 'career' diplomat who devotes a life time to representing his country as an ambassador of good will. In his essay, *The Moral Equivalent of War*, William James made some incisive observations about the psychology of the military mind and its mystical fascination with patriotism, the national honour and war as a permanent ingredient in human life. 'The militarily patriotic and romantic minded everywhere', he wrote, 'and especially the professional military class, refuse to admit for a moment that war may be a transitory phenomenon in social evolution . . . If War had ever stopped, we should have to reinvent it, on this view, to redeem life from flat degeneration.' Referring to two writings, General Homer Lea's *The Valor of Ignorance*, and S. R. Steinmetz's *The Philosophy of War*, James commented, 'militarist authors take a highly mystical view of their subject, and regard war as a biological or sociological necessity . . . readiness for war is . . . the essence of nationality' (pp. 7–8).[19] General Lea's book, written in 1909 and concerned largely with what was then called the 'Yellow peril' or the alleged threat of Japan and China to America's national interest and supremacy in the world, reads like an evangelical tract exhorting all citizens to super-patriotism and military defence of the nation's honour. The 'ignorance' in the title refers to those who refuse to recognise the truth about the nation's peril and suppose that anything short of total military preparedness will be adequate for its preservation. In supporting his ultra-nationalist position, Lea makes much of the need to abandon an 'effeminate' stance, by which he means at the most 'cowards' and 'traitors' and at the least anyone who believes that international tensions and conflicts can be dealt with in any way other than by war. Steinmetz has an equally nationalist orientation, but he places it in a cosmic context; war is the means whereby the 'weak' nations are 'selected out', as

it were, in evolutionary fashion, and the 'strong' nations demonstrate their superiority. James was quite right in saying that these
writers exhibit a 'mystical' view of their subject and that the indissoluble connection between nationalism and war takes on a defin-
itely religious aura.

Hans Kohn in his book, *Prophets and Peoples*, which is a study
of the leaders in nineteenth-century Europe who led nationalist
movements in their respective countries, has called attention to
the zeal with which these leaders invoked religious auspices in
describing the special 'mission' they envisaged for their countries.[20]
Kohn says of Jules Michelet, the major historian and educator of
France in the last century, that of all the interpreters of the French
Revolution, 'None among them has shown a more fervent faith in
its messianic nationalism or a deeper devotion to its democratic
mysticism' (p.43). He quotes from Lamennais's *Paroles d'un Croyant*
(1832) the following dedication:

> What the people will, God himself wills; for what the people
> wills is justice, the essential and eternal order, the fulfillment in
> mankind of that sublime work of Christ. . . . The cause of the
> people is therefore the sacred cause, the cause of God. (p.55)

'Every people', declared Giuseppe Mazzini in his efforts to rally
the Italian nation, 'has its special mission, which will cooperate
toward the fulfilment of the general mission of humanity. That
mission constitutes its nationality. Nationality is sacred' (p.87).
Dostoevsky, who saw himself as the prophet of the Russian mission
to attack the Western Church and Western society, described the
Russian people as 'the bearers of the God on Whom the salvation of
mankind depended' (p.150). It is noteworthy that in each case, God
or the sacred are invoked in behalf of a *national* mission which is at
the same time regarded as essential for the destiny of *mankind* or
humanity.

The idea that a nation has some special 'destiny' in the course of
world history marks the point at which the quasi-religion of nationalism most closely approaches the character – or one of the characters – of what we have been calling the religions proper. 'Destiny',
unlike 'fate' which is generally regarded as an inevitability without
either meaning or purpose, implies some purposeful task or role for
which a nation has been 'called' to carry out. The inhabitants of a
nation that sees itself as having such a destiny believe or are led to

believe that they are in the hands of some higher power which has chosen them for the nation's mission. This mission has taken many forms some of which have had their benign side, but most have proved to be demonic. The image for example, of Puritan America as the 'New Jerusalem' was enormously powerful in its time; America was to be the place where God has gathered people from many lands to make a new beginning in an atmosphere of religious freedom far removed from the intolerance and persecution which was rife in Europe. In itself this vision of a purified faith in which old antagonisms would be left behind was admirable enough, but in time it proved fragile and denominational tensions once again made themselves felt. The vision, nevertheless, was not without its importance in laying the foundations for religious freedom in America. At the opposite end of the spectrum and on a far greater scale was the mission of Hitler's Third Reich which was to last for a thousand years – a deliberate secularising of the Christian symbol of the Millennium – as the bastion of the superior Aryan race which would be sustained by the elimination of all peoples who were guilty of defiling it. To call such a mission by the name of 'nationalism' seems at once too pale and too weak; it was far more than an appeal to German patriotism, but rather a declaration that it was the appointed task of the bearers of the Nazi ideology to dominate not only their own country but the entire world.

A singular feature of Hitler's Nazification programme – it shows itself as a hallmark of all totalitarianism – was its establishment of an intimate connection between the value of the national mission and the aura surrounding the Leader – The *Führer* – who is destined to carry it out. Hence it is not only the nation that is elevated to an object of supreme loyalty for the people, but the apocalyptic power of the Leader as well. Other nations – America, France, Great Britain included – have had national 'missions', but these were often understood as projects which the *nation* itself was fitted to accomplish perhaps over a long period of time and were not tied exclusively to the power of one individual. Hitler, Mussolini, Lenin, and later, Stalin, Castro and Mao represent, in differing degrees, a pattern in which the charismatic leader himself becomes a figure of veneration or of awe mixed with fear and commands an allegiance that transcends even the mission itself. We see this illustrated to the nth degree in the case of Hitler whom one had to address as '*mein Führer*' as if one were acknowledging a saviour or a god. As Julia Ching has pointed out, the same quasi-religious atmosphere pervaded Mao's regime in China where his pictures were placed in Christian places of worship and Christian symbols were removed.

Another form of the idealisation of a nation's destiny is seen in the belief that it embodies some ideal value that other nations should emulate. This belief is exemplified in the Communist ideal of the dictatorship of the working class, the end of the exploitation of one class by another and the overcoming of nationalist aspirations in an international community made up of the oppressed in whatever country they might find themselves. The curious fact in this instance is that, although the Soviet Union was seen as the spearhead in the promotion of Communism, the Marxist ideals had from the beginning an *international* focus and it was only when Russia, especially under the aegis of Stalinism, subordinated these ideals to an intense nationalism that the original appeal of Marx's vision began to erode. Without the belief, however, supported largely by Soviet propaganda, that Communism had actually been achieved in Russia and therefore was a pattern to follow, it is doubtful that Communist parties in other countries such as Cuba, North Vietnam and China would have been able to establish Communist regimes.

Yet another form of national mission is to be found in the belief that a nation has certain cultural values and traditions which should be extended to other peoples as a means of advancing civilisation. Britain's colonialism in the eighteenth and nineteenth centuries which resulted in the formation of the British Empire and its successor, the Commonwealth, belongs to this type. Tillich has described it as 'a Christian humanism for all nations, especially the primitive ones' (Tillich, p.16). and he places this national vocation among a long list of nations which have sought to represent, spread and defend 'a principle of ultimate significance' (ibid.) 'The examples', he writes,

> are abundant: the Hellenic people were conscious of representing culture as against the barbarians; Rome represented the law; the Jews the divine covenant with man; and Medieval Germany the *Corpus Christianum*, religiously and politically. The Italians were the nation of the rebirth (*Rinascimento*) ... France represented the highest contemporary culture; and Russia the saving power of the East against the West; China was the land of the 'center', which all lesser nations encircled. America is the land of the new beginning and the defender of freedom. (ibid.)

Tillich was right, I believe, in his claim that all these vocations have shown both their creative and destructive possibilities; the motives behind the creative intent of these missions is no guarantee against their having destructive consequences, especially when, as has frequently happened, nations lose sight of their vocations and substitute for them a will to power which becomes demonic. The ambiguity of the situation becomes apparent when we realise that no national mission can be significant unless the nation possesses the power to carry it out and thus there arises within the nation a tension between the mission and the power so that, if the mission is a humanitarian one involving many nations, the country continually faces the question whether to use the power to further the cause or to exercise it solely for its own interests and security.

A national mission can become dangerous and pose a threat both to the nation which espouses it and to other nations when the vocation envisaged comes to the national consciousness only gradually and over a long period of time so that when the idea behind the mission emerges in its full clarity and the nation is endowed with power there arises the temptation to become obsessed with accomplishing it. The odyssey of America from the Pre-revolutionary period and the founding of the Republic to the present furnishes an instructive example of the dialectic between mission and power. Stated simply the development was as follows: when America was a weak and struggling nation it espoused and sought to embody ideals of freedom, justice and democracy, ideals which electrified the world and inspired hope in all oppressed peoples. At that stage America appeared as the living experiment and evidence of these ideals, but there had not yet developed the idea that America had a mission to be the defender of freedom; that was to come a century and a half later. When America emerged from the Second World War as the most powerful nation on earth it encountered its first real crisis in wielding of power. Its mission as the major force in defence of freedom and in spreading democracy throughout the world had become a clear part of the American consciousness and the question would now be, how would it use its power.

No one has charted the odyssey of America from its beginnings in the seventeenth-century to the end of the Second World War in the middle of this century with greater insight than Reinhold Niebuhr in *The Irony of American History*. As he pointed out, New England Calvinism and Jeffersonian Deism, great as their differences were, especially about the perfectibility of human nature, joined hands in the belief that America came into being as a 'separated' nation, a nation free of the evils of European feudalism and religious intolerance and possessed of vast spaces in which human aspirations could be realised. The common belief was that God had called America to bring forth a new humanity whether through a new political order or through a 'purer' church – 'God's American Israel', in the words of Yale's President Ezra Stiles. Coupled with this belief were visions of *innocence* and of *virtue*; freedom and democracy were seen not only as a great triumph over tyranny, but also as a climate of innocence within which human beings would no longer participate in the moral corruptions of the Old World. Instead, virtue would abound, even if this was sometimes ascribed to freedom from traditional prejudices and sometimes to favourable social conditions and unlimited (as it seemed) natural resources. Niebuhr's central thesis is that America's sense of difference from – and distance from – the European nations served to re-enforce the belief that we could retain our innocence by refusing to exercise our power except in the interest of a noble cause such as Woodrow Wilson's interpretation of the First World War as a crusade to 'make the world safe for Democracy'. A nation without great power on the world scene may indeed be able to avoid the moral dilemmas and the guilt confronting the use of and misuse of power and the fact that America did not become a world power – at certain points, *the* world power – until after the Second World War was a major factor in preserving its illusion of being innocent and free of the corruptions of 'power politics' as practised by the European nations.

The situation for America in the second half of this century has, of course, radically changed. Whether it is recognised or not, the possession of power carries with it great responsibility, in this case responsibility to a developing world community and under these circumstances America could no longer plead innocent and try to avoid the use of the power thrust upon it. There are, says Niebuhr, two ways for a nation to disavow its responsibilities to the world community, one is *imperialism* and domination and the other is *isolationism*. The latter course was America's chief response to the situation until the advent of the Second World War when that approach became impossible. When America emerged from that war as the most powerful nation on earth it was no longer possible to maintain 'neutrality' and indeed the nation began to see that it must face up to the responsibilities that inevitably accompany such

power. And the curious fact, as Niebuhr reminds us, is that America possessed a moral advantage under the circumstances, since
'No powerful nation in history has ever been more reluctant to
acknowledge the position it has achieved in the world than we'
(Niebuhr, p. 38).

The image of America as the country destined to be the major
force in the extension of democracy throughout the world and the
defender of human rights against totalitarian regimes was both
enlarged and refocused in the light of its confrontation with the
Soviet Union, the second super-power to emerge from the Second
World War. The shooting war gave way to what was known, until
the recent dismantling of the Soviet Union, as the Cold War, a
conflict between two opposed economic and political systems sometimes described as the struggle between the defenders of freedom
and the entire Communist world, and sometimes as the struggle
between Western capitalism and the planned economies of Marxist
oriented countries. This development brought with it a sharpening
of what was seen by many as America's 'mission' – the stamping
out of Communism and the prevention of its spread both in Asia
and in the developing countries of the Third World. The force that
stemmed from America's having had so clear a target becomes
most apparent now that it has been removed.

The world has, of course, altered radically since the time of
Hayes's studies of nationalism. The rise of Hitler and Nazism, of
Mussolini and Italian Fascism, of Stalin and Russian Communism,
of Japan as a modern national state and the culmination of all these
movements in the Second World War have served to intensify the
presence of nationalism and to demonstrate both its force and
the constant threat it poses to peace and what hope there is in the
possibility of a world community. Under these circumstances the
analysis and understanding of nationalist sentiment has had to be
extended to take into account these new and world-shaking phenomena. It is highly significant that a German philosopher and
student of modern culture, Ernst Cassirer, who was forced to flee
from his native land because of the Nazi tyranny should have
added a new dimension to the study of the nationalist state in his
book, *The Myth of the State*. In probing for the sources of those
movements which proclaim the state and its aims as the ultimate
loyalty for all citizens, Cassirer was led to consider the role played
by national leaders – the 'hero' in history – the power of ideas about
a 'pure' race, the impact of the belief in some glorious historical

destiny for a nation and the philosophical foundations of the idea of the state itself. As we shall see, his single contribution to the understanding of nationalism in all its forms is found in his use of a well-founded conception of 'myth' as the means of best expressing the elusive, but starkly real, aura that surrounds the state and bestows upon it a power and authority that knows no bounds.

It is generally agreed that nationalism finds its impetus in some form of projection or symbolic representation of the ideals, the aims and the virtues that define the state and serve as a focus of unconditional allegiance. This projection has been variously described as a doctrine, a conceptual framework, an ideology or an idealisation in the name of which the nationalistic spirit is evoked and sustained. Cassirer grasped this focus of nationalism as a form of myth, what he called the 'myth of the twentieth century' which, of course, includes the myth of the totalitarian state. It is, of course, essential that, as Cassirer knew so well, the term 'myth' not be identified with the corruptions it has suffered in ordinary usage. His studies of mythic expression in many cultures made it impossible for him to accept the use of the term as a synonym for 'false', 'illusory', 'fictional', etc. as has become the practice, especially in polemical writings, of those who condemn the ideas and theories of their opponents as 'mere myths'. For Cassirer, on the contrary, myth is a deep-seated form of expression in human experience which is neither 'primitive' nor confined to so-called 'prelogical' stages in human evolution, but is to be found in all cultures. 'Myth', he writes, does indeed spring from human emotions and affective responses to the world and human life, but is not itself an emotion but the *expression* of emotion, or emotion turned into an image. What was previously only dimly felt takes on through such expression a definite shape.[21]

Central to a proper understanding of myth and its function in social and political life is the distinction Cassirer developed in a number of works between *physical* and *symbolic* forms of expression. The latter is distinctive of man and human culture and differs from animal reactions in that human emotions become more specified and refer to certain classes of objects and do so through symbolic expression which underlies all cultural activities – myth, poetry, language, art, religion and science. While myth often presents us with a fantastic world, a world running counter to ordinary reality, it has, nevertheless in Cassirer's view, a certain objective function, namely, to objectify feelings in a way that differs signficantly from the mere venting of our emotions. In physical reactions there is a sudden explosion followed by a state of rest, so that the emotion spends itself and disappears without a trace. When, however, emotions are expressed in symbolic acts, the situation is quite different. 'In language, myth, art, religion', he writes,

> our emotions are not simply turned into mere acts; they are turned into 'works.' These works do not fade away. They are persistent and durable. A physical reaction can only give us a quick and temporary relief; a symbolic expression may become a *momentum aere perennius.* (pp. 46–7)

Myth, according to Cassirer, is filled with violent emotions and frightful visions, but 'in myth man begins to learn a new and strange art: the art of expressing, that means of organising, his most deeply rooted instincts, his hopes and fears' (p. 48). As we shall see, political myths, including those about the state and nationalism, are perfect vehicles for the expression of those emotions – loyalty, patriotism, hopes and fears – that figure so largely in the promotion of nationalist aspirations. It is important to notice the fact that Cassirer speaks here of myth as an 'art' and one of his most significant perceptions in this regard is that in modern political thought this art has been made into a *technique* or a conscious effort to organise human emotions and orient them toward the aims of the state. Where other writers about nationalism have stressed the 'artificial' character of nationalist doctrine and propaganda, Cassirer explains how myth, not in its original form of religious and moral expression, but in the twentieth-century form of a technique for achieving political ends, can be used to give a definite shape to the human hopes and fears to which national leaders and would-be dictators must appeal if they are to gain control of a people and consolidate their power. They appeal to the hopes of masses of people for security, peace and self-fulfilment and likewise to their fears of a freedom that often proves too burdensome and a responsibility that demands what is beyond their powers. In short, nationalism, and the exaltation of the state as a quasi-god must find expression in ideas and ideals about the virtues and destiny of a nation, on the one hand, and, on the other, these must be accepted with *passion* and *conviction* by the nation's inhabitants. Cassirer's central point is that myth *combines* these two elements essential to the nationalist spirit so as to transcend the situation in which there is on one side an abstract and ineffectual conception of the nation's greatness and power, and, on the other, passions and convictions that lack direction and purpose. Myth, as the symbolic expression of the ingredients of nationalism – worship of the hero, claims to racial superiority and the absolute power of the state – brings together both *purpose* and *power* into a living unity, albeit a potentially demonic one. Cassirer has come closer than anyone else in the way of demonstrating the *shape* of nationalism. The concrete form in which it exists in the minds and hearts of leaders and those who are persuaded, if not coerced, into following them. It is noteworthy, moreover, in view of the important role played by myth in what we have been calling the religions proper, that its presence in the form of the political myth, especially that of the totalitarian state, gives new insight into the way nationalism and statism come to serve as quasi-religions.

The force of nationalism as a substitute for religion becomes even clearer when we consider what Cassirer calls the ingredients of nationalism and his account of their development beginning with the latter half of the last century and ending with the middle of the present one. Cassirer finds three basic ingredients in the nationalism that spawned the totalitarian state – hero-worship of the sort described by Carlyle and also represented by Hegel's 'world historical individuals', belief in a totalitarian race so much popularised in the writings of Gobineau, and certain features of the role of the state in history emphasised by Hegel in his theory of the modern state. Cassirer, it should be noted, is careful to distinguish between the motives of the thinkers who provided these ingredients and the use made of them by the architects of the totalitarian myth. The responsibility for the human horror perpetrated by this myth must fall on the architects and not on those who provided them with their materials.[22]

Not unlike Ralph Waldo Emerson, Carlyle absorbed more German philosophy than he understood and transformed it for his own purpose which was the development of his conception of hero-worship as the mainstay of history. Carlyle found in Goethe a kindred spirit – one of his heroes, to be sure – and was indebted to him for an understanding of nature and art. Goethe however, had no great regard for history and was of little help to Carlyle at the point where he needed it most. For even if, as Cassirer points out, Carlyle had no conception of history as a structured process, history was nevertheless his province and hence he had to turn elsewhere for inspiration. The most likely source would have been the philosopher Herder, often described as the father of German nationalism and a believer in history as the central reality, but Carlyle instead fell under the spell of Fichte's austere metaphysics of duty and action. As Cassirer puts it, Carlyle discovered in Fichte's ethical idealism exactly what he needed: a metaphysics of the hero. For Carlyle, hero-worship represents the oldest and most enduring feature of all social and cultural life and he believed that if all else were to be done away – traditions, creeds, societies – it would remain as mankind's only hope for keeping the world in order. This belief was, for Carlyle, a matter of historical fact; his excursions into German philosophy were for the purpose of transforming it into a theory of heroes and the heroic in history.

Cassirer approaches the central question of what Carlyle understood by a hero and how, as in the case of prophets, a true hero is to be distinguished from a false by pointing to a highly significant shift of emphasis as one passes from the medieval into the modern world. The hierarchical character of medieval life and thought focused on an ascent from the lowest level of Being to the highest, culminating in the worship of God; hero-worship, on the contrary, replaces God with man who, when he is a genuine hero, appears as the representative of the Divine Idea. If, however, we are to test the heroes in order to distinguish the true from the false, some criteria are necessary; as Cassirer points out, Carlyle's mistrust of logic and his penchant for intuitive apprehension in direct experience, led him away from definitions of *what* a hero is and in the direction of illustration showing *who* the great heroic figures were. Carlyle's move in this direction is in perfect accord with his underlying conception of history as a series of *biographies* or the odysseys of those who shaped the course of human life, cultural no less than social and political. The curious fact about this approach is that, on the one hand, the heroic character is said to be one and indivisible, remaining ever the same, but, on the other hand, it is not easy to see what identity runs through the individuals on Carlyle's list – the Norse Odin, Luther, Samuel Johnson, Jesus, Voltaire – nor to understand what he means when he says, 'I hope to make it appear that these are all originally of one stuff'.[23] We gain some insight into his meaning when he speaks of the *artist* in history; the artist is the one who has an 'idea of the Whole' and can understand that only in the Whole can what is Partial be taken for what it is. Cassirer rightly sees that the Whole of which Carlyle speaks is not a metaphysical notion, but an individual whose ideas are known only through knowing the person behind the thinker. The character of the hero is revealed in his *Lebensphilosophie* which includes his 'view of the world'. Man, says Carlyle, joining hands with a number of Enlightenment thinkers, was not made for dealing with the riddle of metaphysics, but for discovering who he is, what his duties are and what his destiny may be. It was in his attempt to answer these questions that Carlyle came to his 'Everlasting Yea', a defiance of death and the affirmation of life in this very defiance. Like William James who applauded the 'yea sayers', Carlyle took something of an heroic stance himself, and declared that the only way to overcome doubt and negativity towards things is not through reflection but through *action*; for Carlyle, ethics supplant metaphysics. Carlyle's philosophy of life had as its capstone the ancient motto, *Laborare est Orare*, and the command 'know thyself' takes on its true meaning when it is translated into, 'know what thou canst work at'.

While Carlyle wrote much about Goethe and his virtues and repeatedly acknowledged his debt to him, especially for *Wilhelm Meister*, there was a great gulf between them on the matter of history. Goethe disparaged knowledge of history and saw it as inferior both to the sciences of nature and to art, while Carlyle saw history as the 'visible garment of God', and great men as the inspired texts of a 'divine book of revelations'. In studying the lives and accomplishments of these men, Carlyle saw himself studying 'the inspired texts themselves'. As we noted previously, he was to find the basic ideas needed for his task in the ethical idealism of Fichte.

Carlyle had not forgotten what he had learned from Goethe about the overcoming of doubt by action, but he was to find this idea developed in a very persuasive way in Fichte's 'The Vocation of Man'. Fichte's discussion, at many points an exhortation, begins with Doubt, proceeds to knowledge and ends with Faith. The main ideas are easily summarised. Approaching the world through theoretical reason leads to the idea of a system of nature thoroughly determined in every respect, including every aspect of human will and action. While, however, this idea satisfies the intellect it contradicts the most profound human aspirations and leaves us powerless to affect our destiny. In short, intellect and will stand opposed; one demands determinism while the other seeks freedom. Echoing Kant's antinomies, Fichte declares that although there is no theoretical ground for deciding between the two, it is impossible to avoid a decision since our peace and dignity are at stake. We end in a state of uncertainty and seek a power to deliver us from it.

In the succeeding section on Knowledge, Fichte sets forth his subjective idealism; we perceive not objects but only the state of ourselves in perceiving things and hence there is no independent material world standing over against us. We need, moreover, no longer be crushed by the idea of the necessity that attaches to that world, because it is a necessity which exists only in our own thought. To complete the argument Fichte insists that knowledge is not reality just because it is knowledge; to see through the illusion is the same as to see that we have within ourselves another access to reality – the will and moral conviction. This is the subject of the third section on Faith where Fichte presents his main thesis about the human condition: 'Not merely *to know*, but according to thy knowledge *to do*, is thy vocation.' Action determines worth. To have purposes and to carry them out is the reason for our being and we have an immediate feeling of an impulse to independent activity which is not created by thought but is itself the foundation of the thought that this is our vocation. All convictions concerning what we are and what we are to do are a matter of faith and proceed from the will and not the understanding. For Fichte, conscience is the root of all truth. It is the task of men of noble conscience to lead humanity to the place where freedom, respect for other beings and peace can be extended throughout the world. 'It is the vocation of our race to unite itself', writes Fichte, 'into one single body, all the parts of which shall be thoroughly known to each other, and all possessed of similar culture' (*Vocation*, Eng. trans., p. 120). What Fichte has in mind is a universal commonwealth in which every useful discovery made in some part of the world will be communicated 'to all the rest' and thus serve the advancement of civilisation. He expresses suspicion of national States in so far as they are not founded in mutual respect for persons and ordered by justice, but seek instead to oppress their citizens and expand their power against other States. He speaks of a *true* State based on human equality and justice and claims that such States will guarantee internal peace and refrain from war with other *true* States. For Fichte we must look to history for the realisation of what reason demands, namely, a commonwealth of free beings who seek to realise themselves and at the same time contribute to the fulfilment of the larger good of humanity. Unfortunately, as Fichte knew well, not everyone has become aware of their individuality and freedom, nor are all possessed of the moral energy needed to advance free-dom and culture in the world. It is to the heroes – those in whom conscience and strength of character abound – that we must turn for leadership.

While Fichte does speak of the heroes as bringing races and tribes together under the dominion of law and justice, he places far more emphasis on the role of the hero in extending *culture* and in making countries 'worthy to be the dwelling-place of cultivated men'.[24] It was in this guise that heroes fascinated Carlyle, and there can be no doubt that what he wrote about them and about hero-worship has played a great part in the development of modern ideas about 'leadership'. Unfortunately, it is equally without doubt that Carlyle's words came to be appropriated by the proponents of modern fascism, but, as Cassirer rightly points out, it is a great mistake to attribute these ideas to Carlyle and for a clear reason. Earlier on, mention was made of the need for criteria to distinguish genuine from sham leaders; Carlyle had such criteria in what he called 'sincerity', and 'insight'. The true hero does not traffic in lies, not even 'noble' ones, and he abhors deception in any form. In addition, the spiritual hero is, above all, a 'thinker' and the poets among Carlyle's heroes – Dante, Goethe, Milton, Shakespeare – are all credited with having suffused their imagination with thought. Nor is that all; what most clearly distinguishes Carlyle's hero from any fascist leader is the *moral force* and the intensity of conviction embodied in the person, the spirit of affirmation over against a negativity which Carlyle repeatedly described as accomplishing *nothing* – in a most literal sense. So sanguine was he in this regard that he did not shrink from declaring that 'might is right' as long as it is 'moral' might that is meant. Carlyle seems to have had, in his own zeal for heroes and hero-worship, something of the virtues he saw in his own heroes, and it is certainly appropriate in a study about quasi-religions to wonder at least whether he had not made his own life-philosophy, his vision of affirming heroes leaving their indelible marks on the history of civilisation, into a quasi-religion to take the place of the Calvinist heritage he had left behind. Whether or not this is true about Carlyle's personal faith, we can be sure that his theory of the hero in history added a powerful ingre-dient to the growth of the nationalism which has dominated this century and which has in its own way presented a serious chal-lenge to the religions proper in the struggle to gain the allegiance of people throughout the world.

In his historical and systematic study of the myth of the state, Cassirer was working backwards, so to speak; starting with the existence of the myth of the totalitarian state in this century, he sought to find its ingredients in past history. We have seen one of the ingredients in Carlyle's theory of hero-worship; two others are located by Cassirer, one in Gobineau's theory of the superior, Aryan race and the other in some features of Hegel's theory of the modern state set forth in his *Philosophy of Right*. As we noted previously, Cassirer, in his characteristic generosity, refrains from holding these three thinkers responsible for what others did with their ideas, although it seems clear that his generous spirit was put to a greater strain in the case of Gobineau than in that of either Carlyle or Hegel.

Gobineau, like the hedgehog in the ancient Greek fable, was in possession of *one* central idea: the inequality of the human races and the supremacy of the white race. In order to lend some credibility to his claim, he found it necessary not only to fabricate history in dealing with some inconvenient facts, but also to undermine all the traditional cultural forms that undergird civilisation – religion, morality, art, patriotism and the state – so as to make room for the one true historical force, the worship of the superior race. Only the white race, Gobineau declared, has the capability of building and sustaining cultural life; the black and yellow races are inferior and lacking in life and energy of their own. As an example of Gobineau's doctoring of history, Cassirer cites the embarrassing fact of the ancient and highly developed Chinese culture which Gobineau could not indeed deny, but which contradicts his theory. Hence he supposed that this culture could not have been the work of the Chinese, but that it must have been created by tribes from India who were presumed to be forerunners of the ancient and 'pure' Aryan race.

To establish his thesis, Gobineau had a formidable task before him. He had to destroy the value of religion, Christianity and Buddhism especially, overturn the universal, philosophically based morality of the Enlightenment philosophers, belittle patriotism and belief in national homogeneity, attack the state as a mere fiction and show the corrupting influence of art. As Cassirer rightly says, race is a jealous god, and will have no other gods before it. In seeking to accomplish his task, Gobineau, as is quite evident, had facile answers for all difficulties and a fertile imagination through which he could supply whatever happened to be lacking in the historical record. Without attempting to outline his endeavour to subvert all values in detail, we may simply indicate the principal ideas that guided his 'arguments'.

According to Gobineau, Christianity is true in a 'metaphysical' sense, but it is impotent when it comes to establishing culture and he went so far as to claim that Christianity had nothing to do with the development of human civilisation.[25] To begin with, the distinction between the 'metaphysical' and the 'cultural' is dubious in itself and it created more problems for Gobineau than he anticipated. The so-called metaphysical aspect of Christianity must certainly include the belief that God created *all* races of human beings and it cannot exclude the ethical ideals of Christianity which are utterly incompatible with Gobineau's theory of a master race. As Cassirer points out, Gobineau's commitment to Christianity led him to be more temperate in his criticism, but in attacking Buddhism as a disaster he shows no restraint whatever. The reason for this attack is quite clear. In denying the caste system – which Gobineau regarded as the means whereby the Aryan race sought to protect itself from 'inferior' blood – the Buddha committed a grave crime against the Aryan race itself, and thus deprived it of its proper force in history.

The idea of universal moral law as set forth by Kant and other thinkers of the Enlightenment was anathema to Gobineau; the superior race can admit no principle that is applicable to *all* peoples, and, moreover, there is no universal man to whom a moral imperative could be addressed. For Gobineau virtue is not a matter of self-determination through freedom; it is solely a matter of blood.

In addition to setting aside religious and moral values, Gobineau had to challenge political ideals as well. The state, he declares, is a fiction and no nation is a homogeneous whole, but only the result of race mixture. The patriotism of the 'native country' is, moreover, not an Aryan ideal since it was never accepted by the Teutonic races, the most noble of the Aryan clan. Patriotism was introduced by the Greeks because of their admiration for the *polis*, but the truth, according to Gobineau, is that the Greeks had inherited it from the Semites – a 'Canaan monstrosity'.[26]

Gobineau realised that he had to come to terms with the world of art and its power to speak to *all* mankind plus the obvious fact that the artistic impulse cannot be supposed to belong to any one race alone. Art, he says, being a product of imagination, is alien to the true Aryan; where, then, does it come from? Gobineau's astounding answer is, from the Negro race. Astounding because, abhorrent as it is, even present day anti-black racism does not fall quite as low as his monstrous depictions of black people – '. . . in their bodily constitution they are below the apes . . . in their brute instincts they are worse than the beasts of prey . . . morally they are on the same level as the evil spirits from hell' (p. 242). For parallels to such vituperation we would have to turn to the Nazi's pictures of the Jews and the dread warnings of the Klu Klux Klan in America against Black people. Despite the patent inconsistencies, Gobineau was undaunted and had the confidence of the fanatic; art had to come from somewhere, but since it came from the black race, true Aryans can have no truck with it. Cassirer has summed up the new race-religion of Gobineau in telling fashion. 'The new religion', he writes,

> the worship of the race, is firmly established; there is no longer fear of any adversary. The Christian religion is ineffective and impotent, Buddhism a moral perversity, patriotism a Canaan monstrosity, law and justice mere abstractions, art a seducer and a prostitute, compassion for the oppressed and pity for the poor sentimental illusions: the list is complete. This is the triumph of the new principle.[27]

The one real agent in world history is the Aryan race; that is the essential message of Gobineau. As soon, however, as he announces it he is forced to conclude that his ideal is self-destructive. The higher races, he admits, cannot rule the world without becoming deeply involved in it, but this is the source of a fatal infection – the mingling of blood – and hence the would-be conquerors must themselves degenerate and end as slaves, a consequence which means at the same time the fall of civilisation since its driving force has been destroyed. What, we may ask, is the deeper message of Gobineau's pseudo-science and manufactured history? It is simply that the god of race reveals itself as no more than an idol of extra-ordinarily demonic proportions. Like all attempts to turn something finite and conditioned into a substitute for God, it must fail. What is finite is unable to bear an infinite burden, and is ill-suited to be worthy of worship; this is a lesson brought home to Western civilisation by the prophets of ancient Israel and its truth has been confirmed ever and again by the most tragic episodes in history. We cannot, however, afford to overlook the aura of the religious which surrounds Carlyle's heroes and Gobineau's Aryans; each approached his god with awe and with the sense of being in the presence of the *Mysterium tremendum* – Rudolf Otto's depiction of the sacred – the 'Divine Idea' which guides all history. Both Carlyle and Gobineau use exalted language when speaking of their gods, language more akin to that of ritual and incantation than to the sober prose of the historian. Both, in short, went very far in the direction of turning heroes and the superior race into objects of quasi-religions and hence we can more readily understand how these ingredients of nationalism and totalitarianism served to establish both as powerful surrogates for the religions proper.

No discussion of modern nationalism and the power of the state can afford to neglect the enormous influence exercised by Hegel's philosophy in this connection, especially his theory of history and the conception of the state set forth in his *Philosophy of Right*. Several decades ago, philosophers, historians and political scientists prompted largely by the regimes of Mussolini, Hitler and Stalin, engaged in an extended and at times bitter debate about the role played by Hegel's political ideas in providing justification for the totalitarian state.[28] Sharply opposed positions were taken up, ranging from Sidney Hook's claim that Hegel's conception of the relation between the state and the individual and his exaltation of the Prussian state were responsible for totalitarianism, to the more measured judgement of T. M. Knox who rejected that view and defended Hegel as an advocate of a justly ordered state whose role is to provide the conditions in which individual freedom becomes *actual* and is no longer merely an ideal. This is indeed no place to reopen that debate, nor would it be profitable to do so, since it is generally agreed that Hegel's writings contain statements which lend some support to both of the views just mentioned and that much depends on what passages are selected and what emphasis is placed upon them.

The first point at the centre of the controversy concerns the doctrine of freedom and Hegel's claim that the *actuality* of freedom and not only the *ideal* depends on the development of appropriate institutions and the social and political conditions through which self-realisation becomes a reality. The threefold development outlined by Hegel in *The Philosophy of Right* starts with the family, passes on to civil society and ends with the state.[29] One of the charges levelled against Hegel – it was first made by Marx in an essay of 1843 – is that freedom is said by Hegel to exist both in the family and in civil society and, as such, forms the basis of the state.

When, however, he comes to define the nature of the state the relationship is reversed and freedom for the individual is seen as derived from or conferred by the state as if it had no antecedent existence. This is indeed a genuine difficulty since Hegel characterised the individual – subjective mind – as a being of reason and freedom and certainly not a creature of the state. If Hegel means that the state 'guarantees' freedom in the sense of maintaining an order of law and justice without which freedom could not flourish, that would be consistent with his claim that the state has the responsibility to bring about the conditions necessary for self-determination. If, however, this guarantee means that the state *bestows* on the individual a freedom which had no prior existence in right, then the situation is quite different and the individual is encompassed by the state in a most fundamental sense.

A more serious problem is posed by Hegel's idea of the 'world spirit' in history and such dramatic statements as 'the state is the march of God through history', or 'the state is the divine Idea as it exists on earth'. These rhetorical statements are translated into something more specific when we consider the consequences of Hegel's sharp distinction between 'morality' – the principles governing the relations between individuals in society – and 'ethical life' in the state (his attempt to translate the *ethos* of the Greek city-state into modern terms). The state, he says, need acknowledge 'no abstract rules of good and bad' so that the will of the state is not bound by morality and if it has any duty whatever it is that of self-preservation *vis-à-vis* other states. Unlike Kant, who had written about 'perpetual peace' among nations to be secured through international law, Hegel insisted on the sovereignty of each state and appealed instead to what he called the judgement of history – 'the history of the world is the world's court of judgement'.[30] The emphasis Hegel placed on sovereignty implies that war between nations is unavoidable and he even saw in such conflict a means of growth in nations and the overcoming of stagnation.

The most disturbing of Hegel's ideas about the universal mind or spirit (*Geist*) in relation to nations in world history is his claim that in each epoch there appears a *dominant* nation which expresses a 'moment' of the Idea that governs history and is such that *no other nations have rights against it*. 'The nation', Hegel writes,

> to which is ascribed a moment of the Idea in the form of a natural principle is entrusted with giving complete effect to it in the

advance of the self-developing self-consciousness of the world mind. This nation is dominant in world history during this one epoch, and it is only once that it can make its hour strike. In contrast with this its absolute right of being the vehicle of this present stage in the world mind's development, the minds of the other nations are without rights, and they, along with those whose hour has struck already, count no longer in world history.[31]

One would have to search far and wide to find a more forceful statement of nationalism gone rampant and it was made by a thinker who himself dominated the philosophical world of the nineteenth century and who claimed for his view no less an authority than that of the world spirit!

There is, however, one feature of Hegel's philosophy which is frequently overlooked and that is unfortunate because it concerns a limit placed upon the power of any state to encompass the individual solely within itself. Hegel's realm of mind has three phases – subjective mind or the individual, objective mind or civil society and the state, and absolute mind represented by art, religion and philosophy. Despite his stray and actually inconsistent references to the state as the 'Divine' in history, the state, for Hegel, belongs to objective mind and *not* to absolute mind, and therefore it is not master of these three spheres. It is not only, as Cassirer says, that art, religion and philosophy have value in themselves and are not to be used by the state for its own ends, but that individuals, being related to absolute mind through artistic creativity, religious faith and the capacity for reflective thought, participate in what *transcends* the state and in this sense are neither its creatures nor its captives. There is something of the legacy of Luther still to be found in Hegel – the demand that we must obey God and not men – and in Hegel's own terms the involvement of individuals with the sphere of absolute mind provides, at least in principle, a bulwark against the absolute authority of the state. Much the same idea has been expressed in the book by Milton Konvitz, *Judaism and the American Idea*, where he points out that the ancient Hebraic idea of human beings as creatures of God is a constant reminder and safeguard against modern, totalitarian nationalism that would make individuals creations of the state.

If we consider the most extreme expressions of nationalism which have made their appearance in this century, whether the Fascism of Mussolini, the Nazism of Hitler or the Communism of Stalin and

Mao, it is not difficult to understand how they have been con-
structed from the ingredients outlined so well by Cassirer – the
worship of the hero in history, the belief in a superior race and the
idea of a state which dominates because it is the bearer of a world
spirit. Not all of these ingredients have figured in the same way and
to the same degree in all these forms of nationalism, but each has
played a significant role in the presentation of the nation state as
the supreme power which demands absolute loyalty and obedience
from those who live within its borders.

We may summarise the preceding discussion and thus express its
upshot by focusing on some reasons why nationalism can never be
more than a quasi-religion. Even though nationalism evokes intense loyalty and demands an unconditional commitment to its
ideals for a nation, expresses itself in a rhetoric that goes far beyond
the sober prose either of history or political philosophy, and cele-
brates its heroes, sacred events and places with a solemnity that
approaches the religious, it, nevertheless, has no resources for dealing with those personal human needs and concerns to which the
religions proper address themselves. There are at least six points
at which nationalisms show themselves to be deficient; first, and
most basic, is the elevation of a *finite* and conditioned reality to an
absolute status; second, the nation as an object of supreme loyalty
is an *impersonal* god even when it reflects the personality of a
charismatic leader; third, the nation has no *vision of individual self-
fulfilment* and of the life that is most worthy of living apart from its
demand that one live, and perhaps die, for the national honour;
fourth, the nation as such knows nothing of the meaning of personal despair, guilt, forgiveness, repentance and all the problems
described by William James under the heading of the *'divided self'*;
fifth, the nation bent on pursuing its nationalist aspirations can
have no place for the *self-critical* voice of the prophet who warns
against arrogance and knows the value of humility; sixth, in all its
many manifestations, nationalism is *divisive*, setting nation against
nation, people against people in a self-righteousness that knows no
bounds.

Before explaining these points in more detail, a word of caution is
in order. It would be a folly that I am not about to engage in to
ignore the fact that the religions proper have ever been subject to
corruption; on the contrary, the very ultimacy that attaches to God
or the supremely worshipful reality and at the same time reveals
the gulf between the Sacred and the waywardness of mortal flesh

always makes possible *demonic* distortion; avowedly *religious* wars are more terrible than any other conflicts because of the conviction that the *really* Ultimate is at stake. In this respect, there can be no surprise in the discovery that quasi-religions should themselves be subject to the same distortions to be found in the religions proper. In quasi-religions, however, we find demonic distortion at the root which is the reason that I have singled out as the first and most basic deficiency of nationalism – as in all quasi-religions – the elevation of a finite and conditioned reality to an *absolute* status. It is there that the idolatry falls.

No creation by human beings can serve as the ground of all there is, both that it is and the way it is; such creations are all finite, limited and subject to corruption. The state or nation is no exception; as we have seen, for all of its roots in 'natural' bonds between people, the modern nation state is itself the work of human *artifice* and nationalistic claims represent a further extension of human ingenuity. One thinks here of the scathing attack made by the prophet Isaiah on the worshipping of idols, graven images made out of wood by human hands. While the state, to be sure, is no graven image, the analogy is close enough to expose the folly in turning the state, a human artefact, into an object of absolute devotion. Even those who, like the biblical fool who said there is no God, should not compound their folly by elevating the state to the rank of the divine.

The state, in contrast to the dominant character of God as envisaged by the Western religions, is *impersonal* in character and even if personal terms have been used for the state – 'she', 'fatherland' – it is inconceivable that the state could ever be regarded as a 'Thou'. A personal element enters in only to the extent that a charismatic leader is seen as the *embodiment* of the nation's aspirations and it is in this sense that a hero is more readily deified than a country.

As a socio-political institution, the state can have no vision of individual self-fulfilment or an ideal of the life that is most worth living such as we find in the traditional religions. Even when the attempt is made to project such a vision as in the case of Communism and Democracy the ideal remains external and is geared to political survival. The experience of Socrates makes this patently clear. What, the authorities asked, was he doing with his idea of self-knowledge and the examined life, but undermining the foundations of the political order?

The state has no resources for dealing on a personal level with those intimate concerns to which the traditional religions speak.

Nationalist aspirations have nothing to say to the cycle of transgression, guilt, repentance and forgiveness so well known to the religious consciousness and beyond the call to patriotism and the national honour the nation has no way of overcoming the predicament of the 'divided self' which does what it knows it should not, and fails to do what it should.

One feature of the traditional religions which is invariably overlooked, especially by critics, is the self-critical, prophetic and reforming voice raised from within the tradition itself against idolatry and corruption. Large portions of the Jewish and Christian scriptures are devoted to a condemnation of religion itself when it has gone astray, following false gods fostering arrogance and betraying its highest ideals. Nationalism, in the nature of its self-confident pride, can brook no critics and is quick to brand any dissident voice with the mark of the traitor.

Finally, as every student of nationalism has pointed out, it is inevitably a divisive force. Even when, as we have seen, nationalist movements have sought to connect their cause with the welfare of humanity or of mankind, the broader vision is subordinated to the narrower demands of the nation, and the reason is clear: nationalism can live only when it means the elevation of a nation over other nations. By contrast, the traditional world religions have projected an ideal which transcends all national and ethnic boundaries in a vision of unity and peace embracing all mankind. That this ideal has not been realised is patent, but it remains at least a matter of principle and one that is lacking in every nationalism.

5

Retrospective Summary

The upshot of the foregoing study of Humanism, Marxism and Nationalism is their identification as what I have been calling 'quasi-religions' as distinct from the commonly acknowledged world religions such as Buddhism and Christianity. The reason for classifying quasi-religions under the heading of religion is that they do offer a supreme object, value or ideal which calls forth dedication and devotion and which serves as a way of integrating the self and of providing an over-arching purpose for life, a purpose for which in some cases people are even willing to die. It is in view of these features that quasi-religions are capable of performing some at least of the functions associated with the religions proper, something that explains why quasi-religions come to compete with the world religions and often seek to replace them. The point can be sharpened by a comparison with what used to be called the 'warfare' between religion and science. The truth is that science, whether in the form of a pattern of inquiry or a body of knowledge, is not fitted to take the place of religion in human life, whereas the quasi-religions have the resources and sometimes the aim of establishing themselves as substitutes for the historic religious faiths. Such substitutes come closer to the religions proper than any form of science could possibly come, and hence they are rivals to be reckoned with.

What then is the force of the 'quasi' in describing the quasi-religions? The answer is clear; the qualifier indicates that the object, value, ideal commanding an ultimate allegiance – humanity, the nation-state, the classless society, the necessary dialectic of history – is something *finite* and *conditioned* which, like all such realities, is subject to corruption and idolatry. The absolutising of what in itself is no more than a finite part of the natural world or some particular facet of the cultural world opens the way to the demonic destructiveness that stands opposed to a truly divine love, beauty and creativity. We see this truth in a way at once ironic and tragic in the ancient Greek mythology. Zeus was acknowledged to be the first among the gods of the Pantheon, but he was tainted by finitude in

having a *fate* which meant that he, though 'immortal', was subject
to a power beyond himself – the power of fate (*Moira*), always
symbolised by the iron chains of *necessity*. Thus Zeus was not
ultimate; the Absolute beyond his power was that of Fate itself and
the irony was revealed through several centuries of Christian history where the false absolutising of Fate was finally overcome in
the idea of divine Providence.

On several previous occasions attention was called to the nature
of religion as a pervasive fact of history and as a distinctive dimension of human experience which manifests itself in the concern to
find an Ultimate which, in turn, is the answer to the question of
life's purpose. What have been called the religions proper – Christianity, Judaism, Buddhism – represent particular and historically
rooted apprehensions of the reality that fulfils the religious quest
and is the supreme focus of devotion. It was further proposed that
these religions exhibit a *general pattern* that is threefold, starting
with a *diagnosis* of the human predicament, of actual human existence, made by comparing that existence with the nature of the
religious Ultimate – Love, Justice, Mercy – for the purpose of determining what is wrong about us and what stands in the way of
achieving an ideal fulfilment. This perception of 'something wrong'
about us, the sense that life is out of joint as it naturally exists, leads
to the quest for a power that can *deliver* us from this wrongness.
William James in *The Varieties of Religious Experience*, put this point
in an arresting way. In expanding his claim that 'there is a certain
uniform deliverance in which religions all appear to meet' (*Works*,
Harvard Ed., p.400), James says, '(there) is a sense that there is
something wrong about us as we naturally stand, and 'The solution is
a sense that *we are saved from the wrongness* by making proper
connections with the higher powers' (ibid.).

James, it is important to notice, was not proposing this common
ground among religions as a conjecture or a theory, but rather as an
observation borne out by the facts and in accord with what religion
shows itself to be.[1] The concern of all religions for deliverance,
salvation (literally, 'being made whole again'), release, liberation
and enlightenment is a hallmark and a pervasive feature that remains constant in the midst of very considerable differences as to
the nature of the deliverance and, correlatively, what it is that we
need to be delivered from. As we have seen, even Zaehner who lays
great stress on the *discordant* features in his study of the world
religions, acknowledges that there is common ground to be found

in the fact that providing release stands at the centre of them all. And I would insist again that this fact is not to be ignored nor minimised in its importance because of the errors and false aims to be found in decades of work in the area known as 'comparative religion'. Efforts at 'harmonising' the world religions were clearly misguided and this is also true, as Zaehner rightly points out, of attempts to interpret one religion in terms of another. These failures, however, must not lead us to overlook what common ground actually exists in the form of the common concern for deliverance from the evils inherent in the human situation.

An illuminating way to understand the quasi-religions is to see to what extent they exhibit the general pattern previously spelled out. What is their diagnosis of the human situation? What is their conception of the evils or the 'flaw' in human beings which needs to be overcome? What is the means of deliverance? The appeal to the general pattern in religions, it must be understood, has its limitations since it is easier to apply to Marxism and to Humanism than is the case with Nationalism with its protean character. There is, however, one point which has been emphasised on numerous occasions where the comparison is directly relevant for all three quasi-religions and that is the basic nature of the religious Ultimate. It is clear that for the religions proper that Ultimate can be nothing finite, whereas it is equally clear that for the quasi-religions what is acknowledged to be Ultimate is a finite reality devoid of mystery, public, open to inspection or 'profane' in its original meaning.

Let us attempt to review the answers given by the quasi-religions to the above questions posed by the pattern in religions, starting with Humanism. To begin with, for most forms of Humanism, in contrast to Judaism and Christianity where the flaw in human nature is found in human self-assertiveness or rebellion against God, there is no such wholistic diagnosis of the human predicament. The obvious reason is, of course, that there is no belief in God, but something more is involved. Humanism finds no one fundamental flaw in human nature and certainly not one that cannot be overcome by human resources, but looks instead to particular evils and errors such as ignorance, superstition, injustice, fanaticism, dogmatism and indeed all of the shortcomings of human beings in a civil society. According to Humanism: these are the obstacles standing in the way of the fulfilment of the talents and capacities of everyone in this world. Overcoming them, howsoever difficult, is believed to be within the power of human resources;

man is his own deliverer. Lamont, as we have noted, made this claim explicitly in his Fourth article of Humanism: 'Humanism believes that man has the power and the potentiality of solving his own problems successfully, relying primarily on reason and scientific method to do so and to enlarge continually his knowledge of the truth' (pp. 16–17). Reason and science, together with moral education, the humanising influence of the arts and democratic forms of government are the principal means whereby the Humanist ideal of a universal order of peace, justice and brotherhood is to be achieved. In accordance with his all-embracing Naturalism and his optimism with regard to human powers, Lamont sees nothing in mankind's capacity for injustice, deception and corruption which cannot be overcome by the means he has cited. It is at this point that his form of Humanism stands in the sharpest contrast to biblical religion where the fundamental flaw in man is in his misuse of freedom and in his setting himself up as his own end. If it is not too paradoxical, the contrast can be seen most clearly when it is cast in theological terms. Christianity has always distinguished between 'sin' as the state of being estranged from God and 'sins' as those particular wrongful deeds and thoughts which follow from that estrangement. Lamont can acknowledge only the particular misdeeds, since he has no belief in any pervasive propensity or tendency in man to commit them. Reason, for him, and science are regarded as unambiguously good and if he were to acknowledge that both can and have been used for evil ends, he would have to claim that these misfortunes could be conquered only by the further application of these same means.

The emphasis in Humanism on particular evils in human conduct and in the world as purely natural facts standing in need of no general explanation has repercussions for the 'problem of evil' focused by biblical religion in its concern to understand something of the mystery of evil, both its presence in the world and the particular beings it affects. For Humanism, there is and can be no such thing as 'the' problem of evil in a wholistic sense, because it acknowledges no more than the existence of *evils* and, in fact, Lamont lists among these evils the theological problem of evil itself. He sees the issue as posed by the Book of Job and by the tradition of theodicy, philosophical as well as theological, as the transformation of a natural fact into a mystery beyond human comprehension. Dewey expressed much the same view in his book, *A Common Faith*, where he claims that there are problems of evils aplenty, but he eschews involvement in 'the' problem of evil on the grounds that it is insoluble and, further, grappling with it diverts attention and energy away from attacking the evils that exist. Whatever difficulties there are in the effort to 'justify the ways of God to man', the fact remains that biblical religion was responding to the deeply rooted human concern for some kind of understanding, however dark, for some form of meaning in the evils that beset us. Many years ago I discussed this concern with a member of the old Vienna Circle of philosophers and, not surprisingly, he proposed to answer the question of the anguished mother, 'Why did my son die?' with the matter of fact, 'Because his heart stopped beating'. I responded by saying that, of course, we know that, but it clearly leaves something essential out. How is it, I asked, that we both know in a human and commonsensical way that the 'why' of the mother's question in not the 'why' of the answer given? He agreed, but went on to say that the ultimate 'why' question cannot be answered in terms of empirical knowledge and hence has to be regarded as 'meaningless' even though, speaking as a human being, he was prepared to admit that he understood what the person was asking. Although Christianity has never denied, in opposition to some forms of Gnosticism and Docetism, the natural fact of death and the evils in the world, it has continued to follow the instincts of the biblical Job whom, it will be recalled, was convinced against all advice to the contrary, that there *is* an answer to his petition even if it is hidden in the inscrutable ways of God.

Another point of contrast, one that has its own irony, appears in Lamont's treatment of death and immortality. On his view, the desire for a future life is necessarily connected with belief in a Divine Being having the power to bring it about, and hence the issue between Humanism and supernaturalism is that between mortality and immortality. Lamont's contention is that the body and the personality (sometimes called the 'mind') grow together and die together; personality does not survive the death of the body. So sanguine is he in his insistence on the indissoluble connection between body and personality that he invokes the Christian idea of 'resurrection' as re-enforcing that very connection. That is correct as far as it goes; neither Judaism nor Christianity envisaged the human person as disembodied or identical merely with the 'mind'. The irony, however, and I will not deny that the error has often been made by Christian thinkers confused by the idea of 'natural religion' stemming from the Enlightenment, is that the image of resurrection represents classical Christian doctrine, while the idea of immortality does not. Immortality implies a never-ending continuation of the same sort of life we already know, and is an essentially *quantitative* notion. On the contrary, the image of resurrection – I say 'image' because we obviously do not know and Paul prefaces his comments about it by saying, 'Behold, I tell you a mystery' – is a *qualitative* one implying a new person and a new body on a new level of being; it is not to be thought of as merely 'more of the same'. There is no essentially religious significance in the idea of an everlasting continuation of mortal existence without qualitative change. The image of resurrection expresses the idea of a spiritual transformation – from a 'natural' body to a 'spiritual' body – which is altogether absent from the idea of immortality. Reinhold Niebuhr was right in his contention that immortality seems more 'rational' with its ancient roots in Plato's thought than the image of resurrection with all its vagueness. The truth is that the stress placed by biblical religion on the unity of the body and the person is precisely what makes the idea of immortality unsuitable, since all versions of that doctrine involve the belief that only a *part* of the being lives on, that part being, since the days of Plato, the 'immortal' part, namely, the mind. In consequence, Lamont's criticism should be directed not so much against the 'supernatural' – by which he usually means Christianity – as against the entire, largely philosophical, tradition of arguments for immortality.

Humanism reveals itself as a quasi-religion in the most perspicuous way when we consider how closely it fits the general pattern of religions to which we have appealed on numerous occasions, albeit in largely secular terms. Using an ideal image of man, his potentialities and powers, his reason, energy, determination and ingenuity, as a standard, Humanism makes a diagnosis of the actual situation and finds that multiple obstacles stand in the way of man's becoming what he ideally may become. These obstacles are by now familiar, consisting essentially in vices long known to reformers and moralists supplemented by a new evil, namely, religion that allegedly denigrates man and his powers by appealing to 'supernatural' powers for deliverance. Two errors are said to be involved; the first is belief in the supernatural which Humanism regards as illusory, and the second is the belief that the very appeal to such powers implies the inability of man to overcome the evils found in human beings and in society. Thus Humanism includes a disclosure of what stands in the way of man's ideal fulfilment as compared with man as he ought to be and a quest for what will set things right. As noted previously, that quest is short because it is found in present human resources – scientific knowledge, especially as applied to social and political issues, *control* of history through technology, moral integrity, aesthetic sensitivity and democracy both as a form of government and as a way of life. The point most to be emphasised here is that Humanism (with the possible exception of 'religious' Humanism) finds no evil, no error, no obstacle in the human situation which cannot be overcome through the power and the effort possessed by human beings as they actually exist. It is this point where all the varieties of Humanism stand in the sharpest contrast to Christianity and the other religions proper. It is interesting to note that James called Buddhism and Christianity the most 'profound' religions because of their recognition of the depth of evil and their appreciation of how intractable it has proved to be throughout history. We are back to the paradox seen by all the religions proper, namely, how is the same being who needs to be delivered from evils many of which are due to the misuse of freedom, able to deliver himself?

As a concluding note, no discussion of Humanism can avoid the problems stemming from the ambiguity of the term itself and the wide range of positions it has stood for. As we have seen, there is the Humanism that aims to keep itself on purely secular ground and sets itself against the supernatural. But then there are those whose basic sympathies are with this type of Humanism but who want to broaden it to include a religious dimension because they are not satisfied with the Naturalism and the scientism so prominent in the Humanism of Lamont. To complicate the picture further, Jacques Maritain, the eminent Catholic thinker, described his position as an 'integral humanism' which obviously does not exclude religion and on numerous occasions the Catholic Church has insisted that Christianity is a humanism based on God. The scholars of the Renaissance who sought to recover the legacy of the Graeco-Roman civilisations called themselves Humanists and, although they paid more attention to man's creative than to his destructive powers, they did not see themselves as enemies of Christianity. It is obvious that Christianity in all its forms has a central concern for the welfare and destiny of man epitomised in Christ who was called both Son of God and Son of Man. In this sense it embraces a humanism. The dividing line, however, comes at the point where Humanism denies God, recognises no power in the universe but that of man and sets itself up as a replacement of Christianity. It is in this sense that the Humanism we have discussed shows itself to be a quasi-religion.

Turning now to Marxism, let us summarise the main points made previously, especially in connection with the parallels between Marxism and Christianity. To begin with, Marxism has its own diagnosis of the human predicament, its vision of deliverance and its prophetic and apocalyptic elements, all combined with the rejection of any transcendent reality. This diagnosis is twofold; first, for Marx, man as he actually exists is alienated from himself because of an unjust socio-economic system which exploits his labour and reduces him to a thing. Second, religion itself is a source of alienation because it fosters the illusion that man revolves about God, whereas the truth is that man should revolve around himself and, like Humanism, be his own end. It is important to notice that in declaring the alienation of man, Marx was using as a standard for comparison his vision of the new man in the new society where alienation has been overcome. There is thus a prophetic and even an apocalyptic side to Marx's thought which distinguishes it from the one-dimensional view of Humanism. But, again like Humanism, it sets itself against the Judeo-Christian tradition in denying God and establishing man as the centre of the universe.

Having identified the causes of alienation, Marx had then to find the means of deliverance, the forces that do away with alienation and lead to a social order in which human beings recover their true humanity. As we have seen Marx envisioned several means of deliverance working together to bring about the triumph of the classless society. One is the power of the Proletariat to create revolutionary conditions resulting in the overthrow of the capitalist system. Another is the dialectic of history working in a necessary way and leading to the inevitable outcome which is nothing less than the creation of the new human being and the founding of an international order based on justice and freedom. The basic faith in the view that history 'is on our side' and thus assures the triumph of Marx's vision was one of the most attractive features of the appeal enjoyed by the political Communism spawned by his thought. The third means of deliverance brought about by Communism was the Communist Party itself and its robust faith that any means however evil can and must be used to foster Communist goals. The idea was that although men become evil in the service of the good cause, when it is accomplished they will be transformed.

From a biblical perspective such a faith is no more than an illusion. How did it happen that a faith which rejected belief in the transformation of man through love and trust in God envisioned by Christianity came to embrace belief in an apocalyptic change in human beings to be brought about by a new socio-economic order? I find this a conundrum; if there is any explanation, it is probably to be found in the common human tendency manifested by those whose main aim is to destroy the illusions of others to harbour illusions of their own without realising the contradiction.

The role played by Marxism (Communism) as a quasi-religion or a substitute for the Judeo-Christian tradition, is vividly illustrated by the personal experiences recounted in *The God that Failed*. Arthur Koestler's odyssey furnishes the most explicit evidence and it is confirmed at important points by the other writers. Koestler, it will be recalled, spoke of how little difference there is between a 'traditionalist' and a 'revolutionary' faith; both are zealous in their attack on the existing order in the name of an ideal derived from the *past* – the primitive Christian communities standing against the power of the Roman State and the primitive Communist society envisioned by Marx and Engels as having existed at the 'beginning' of the dialectic of history – and projected into the *future* as a goal to be recovered. Koestler describes the impact that the Communist faith had upon him and speaks of his having become a 'convert' to it, firm in the belief that it had 'grasped' him in a way more powerful than the force of a deliberate choice. Koestler, moreover, was most perceptive in seeing the similarity between the Party and a church; the former, he wrote, is not like a club or even an ordinary political party which one joins or resigns from at will because it demands an absolute loyalty and offers a fulfilment for the human need to feel significant and useful even under the worst conditions.

Equally striking as an indication of the quasi-religious character of the Communist movement is the powerful symbolism through which its chief concerns were expressed. History, World Revolution, the Proletariat take on special significance as determiners of human destiny. History is no mere order of events, but, as we have seen, *the* medium ordained to bring about the new order; World Revolution is no ordinary uprising having a date like the French Revolution or the American, but is seen in apocalyptic terms; the Proletariat is no ordinary class of workers but is *the* group that bears the cause of humanity itself in the dialectic of history. Similarly, a quasi-religious aura was associated with the heroes of Communism – the statues of Lenin, the great pictures of Stalin in Russia, of Castro in Cuba and of Mao Zedong in China – as a means of evoking loyalty to the cause. Mao, as Julia Ching records in the events of the Cultural Revolution, went beyond the mere criticism of both Buddhism and Christianity and sought to replace them with symbols of his own. Thus domestic shrines were destroyed and pictures of Mao were put in their place, red flags replaced crosses in Christian churches and bibles were burned. The chief aim of these practices was the establishment of Mao as the ultimate object of devotion and as the replacement of God and the Buddha. One might say that, in view of these overt attacks on Christians and Buddhists, Maoism was unique in going beyond being a quasi-religion and becoming a full-fledged religion in its own right. Whatever the future may hold in store for Communism in China, we have before us, in addition to the dismantling of the Soviet Union, the compelling testimony of the authors of *The God that Failed*; they stood ready to put Communism in the place of God, but they discovered subsequently that the object of their new found faith was merely an idol. Their experience told them that they had invested in no more than a quasi-religion.

In turning now to Nationalism, I shall endeavour to highlight those points at which nationalisms have sought to appropriate certain features of traditional religion for their own ends and thus to supplant these religions. In addition, I shall emphasise those elements in Nationalism which have proved to be basically demonic. To begin with, Hayes's account of Nationalism as a 'religion' in its own right must be taken seriously, even if, as he was aware, there are human religious concerns and needs which Nationalism is ill-equipped to meet. As we have seen, Nationalism has spawned new gods – Progress, Perfectionism, Science, Humanity, The Fatherland – and these in combination with national interests have served as objects of unconditional loyalty which hitherto was the prerogative of the biblical God. It is important to notice that the underlying development was the transposition of the *sacred* from its place in Christianity and the other world religions, to the cult of the nation, its leaders, its symbols – national hymns and anthems, flags, seals, founding documents and declarations, commemorative dates and places – and, finally, its ideal view of itself as standing for some special virtue or of its having a mission in world history. The appropriation of the sacred by the nationalistic aspirations of the state has taken place with respect to persons, heroes, leaders, symbols such as flags and intangibles such as the honour of the nation, an honour which frequently is called 'sacred honour' in times of war. We have seen illustrations of all of these appropriations of the sacred in the preceding discussion of Nationalism. Here we may summarise with typical examples.

The most striking case of the national leader taking on a sacred aura is, of course, Adolf Hitler. He not only demanded absolute allegiance to himself and to the cause of the Fatherland, but he personalised the relationship by insisting on being addressed by individuals as *mein Führer* as if he were a kind of saviour or even a god in human guise. That is Nationalism going beyond itself and assuming the mantle of religion, that is, quasi-religion. Mao, it appears, was not far behind in this sort of appropriation of the sacred. He filled domestic Buddhist shrines with pictures of himself – a secular ikon – and he replaced crosses in Christian houses of worship with red flags and other Maoist symbols. Both figures represent Carlyle's cult of the hero, but without the redeeming features which he believed true heroes possess.

In the case of symbols such as national flags or banners the transposition of the sacred is especially significant because it is twofold. The national flag is *the* sacred symbol of the nation as a whole, expressing its actualities, its possibilities and its aspirations. The salute or some form of homage paid by an individual to the flag is the sign of total allegiance to the country for which the flag stands. The flag not only as a symbol but as a physical object comes to take on a power and a meaning all its own, hence the elaborate rules prevailing in almost all countries concerning the display of the flag, when it is to be flown, how it is to be folded, what desecrations are prohibited such as stepping on the flag or burning it, etc. Let us consider briefly two counterparts in the Christian tradition – the Bible and the Cross (also the Crucifix) – whose roles may be compared with that of the flag. Both the Bible and the Cross share the twofold character of the flag; they are symbols pointing beyond themselves to God, the first as the divine Word and the second as the sacrificial love of Christ. They are also like the flag, physical objects, although the Bible or any other sacred Scripture since they are texts can never be regarded solely as a physical object. There is, however, a crucial difference between the national symbol and the religious symbols; the latter are not themselves 'divine' but rather point beyond themselves to the God whose being they express and the churches have had continually to stress this fact in prophetic criticism of the human tendency to elevate these symbols in an idolatrous way so that they come to supplant the divine reality to which they bear witness. The question is, are there resources within the state represented by the flag for teaching its citizens not to turn the flag itself into an idol? If the Bible and the Cross are not God, the flag is not the nation.

The main reason why the nationalist state has great difficulty in exercising the prophetic criticism against idolatry – and there *is* secular idolatry – is that it recognises in most instances no power of judgement beyond itself. The Christian Churches may not always have succeeded in avoiding idolatry, both with Bible and Cross, but the prophetic criticism is there as a constant warning and indeed without it idolatry could not have been unmasked in the first place. The problem facing all quasi-religions is the absence of any awareness that their own absolutes are also subject to judgement, whether of God or, as Hegel believed, of world history.

It is curious in the extreme that the modern secular mind to which traditional religion appears as superstitious and outmoded should be so quick to wrap the mantle of the sacred around the patriotic symbols that express the past, present and hoped-for future of the national state. As was noted previously, national holidays in every country are celebrated – the term itself has its 'home', as Wittgenstein would say, in religious ritual – with solemnity and awe, as is also the case with the birthdays of national heroes and Founding Fathers, and special historic events from the nation's past. In this regard, one of Hayes's most telling examples is the fact that many people who have long rejected the idea of the human 'soul', have no hesitation in speaking about the 'soul' of the nation on ceremonial occasions. Perhaps the only explanation for this transposition of the sacred is that, while the things of religion appear intangible and elusive, the state and its trappings are present for all to see. And yet this is not wholly true, because nationalism most often feeds not on a picture of a nation as it actually exists, but on the ideals and aspirations it envisages and, most important of all, the mission it has in history. Christianity has often spoken of the Celestial City as a 'City out of sight', but we need to remember that nationalism is based, like Hitler's Third Reich that was to stand for a thousand years, on a nation that, too, is out of sight.

Attention has been called to the demonic distortions that arise when something finite is elevated to the status of an absolute in whose name 'all is permitted'. By far the most destructive of these distortions within the scope of Nationalism is the belief – it has taken many forms – in a 'pure' or 'master' race supposed to have power over the rights of all other peoples. The force of the evil in this belief must be seen in three dimensions: the scientific, the religious and the historical. It is generally agreed that, from a scientific standpoint, there is no such thing as a 'pure' race; all peoples are amalgams of many ethnic groups. Gobineau's pseudo-scientific attempt to establish the existence and the priority of an 'Aryan' race has been shown to be entirely false. The fine analysis by Cassirer of Gobineau's flawed method, his dubious assumptions and, especially, his doctoring of history clearly establishes the folly of his effort. The existence of Chinese civilisation and of the cultures of the African peoples, as Gobineau knew but chose to ignore, present monumental anomalies for which his racial scheme is totally unable to account. Unfortunately, the discrediting of even such a conspicuous attempt to establish the existence of a 'pure' race or a national race has not banished the idea itself and we see it at work in Bosnia and other parts of the world at the present time.

The appeal to race often accompanying Nationalism runs directly counter to Christianity's basic beliefs concerning man and God, and in two senses. First, according to Christian faith, race as such is totally invalid as a criterion for determining the worth of human beings and hence, *a fortiori*, equally invalid is a claim made in behalf of any particular ethnic group. When the New Testament declares that 'in Christ there is neither Jew nor Greek', we are to understand that human beings have worth and dignity in the sight of God not on the basis of race, but solely in virtue of the fact that they are human persons. This is not to deny the reality of ethnic identity, but rather to insist that such identity has nothing to do with the being of the person in the eyes of God.

It is a well-known fact of history that the Christian view came to prevail in the West and it is quite ludicrous that Gobineau should have tried to do away with this fact by his quite absurd distinction between the 'metaphysical' and the 'cultural'. As we have seen, he used this distinction to claim that Christianity is true in the metaphysical sense, but that it had nothing to do with the development of civilisation. Apart from this blatant disregard of history, Gobineau's own distinction turned out to be a snare because the so-called metaphysical aspect of Christianity must certainly include the doctrine that God created *all* the peoples of the earth thus precluding any idea of a master race in whatever way it is defined.

How seductive but also demonic the idea of a 'pure race' can be becomes clear in Gobineau's treatment of Buddhism. He envisaged the caste system as the means for protecting the Aryan race from 'inferior' blood and hence the Buddha, in rejecting that system, is said to have committed a grave crime against the race destined to be the major force in history.

The most cruel and destructive consequence of absolutising racial purity is that it leads, as it must, to *genocide*. The elimination of those whose blood is 'impure' is seen as the only guarantee against pollution. We saw this happen in the Holocaust where the murder of the Jewish People was described as Hitler's 'final' solution, 'final' being the operative word here because it shows that the ideology of racial purity can be realised only in genocide. We see the same thing happening at present in the 'ethnic cleansing' carried out by the Serbians in their effort to eliminate the Muslims.

As has been so often stressed, the hallmark, but also the fatal flaw, of quasi-religions is that their ultimate objects demanding absolute loyalty are finite and conditioned realities elevated to the status of an absolute. The humanity or mankind of Humanism, the inescapable dialectic of history in Marxism and the all-encompassing state of Nationalism share this characteristic feature. From the standpoint of the Judeo-Christian tradition these absolutes are all idols standing under the prophetic judgement so well expressed by Isaiah when he warned against worshipping graven images made of wood by human hands. From that same standpoint, Humanism, Marxism and Nationalism are all to be seen as 'the gods that failed'.

Notes

1: THE RELIGIONS PROPER AND QUASI-RELIGIONS

1. Paul Tillich, *Christianity and the Encounter of the World Religions* (New York and London: Columbia University Press, 1963) pp. 4–5.
2. See R. C. Zaehner, *Concordant Discord* (Oxford: Clarendon Press, 1970) pp. 176–7.
3. Zaehner, *Concordant Discord*, p. 11. There is yet another parallel in the 'Great Ultimate' of the neo-Confucians.
4. Tillich, *Christianity and the Encounter of the World Religions*, p. 64.
5. It has never been clear to me why James thought that this task defines *the* relation of philosophy and religion; philosophy is clearly involved in what he proposed, but it is clear that the enterprise is primarily *historical* in character and certainly does not exhaust the role of philosophy in this connection.
6. Many of those who reject religious ultimates do so firm in the belief that they have simply put the matter aside; it has, however, an annoying tendency to reappear. An excellent example is found in the case of Voltaire who vigorously objected to histories written from a religious point of view and divine providence, claiming that this was no more than dogmatism and superstition. When, however, he set out to write his history he did so from the standpoint of his Enlightenment ideals – progress, objective truth and the death of superstition – and thus substituted one ultimate for another. It is not necessary to claim that all ultimates are justified in order to hold that from *some* ultimate there is no escape. The real danger about ultimates is not their existence, but the self-deception involved when people have ultimates but refuse to admit it.
7. Tillich, *Christianity and the Encounter of the World Religions*, p. 5.
8. Reinhold Niebuhr has dealt with this matter in brilliant fashion in his chapter 'The Master of Destiny', in *The Irony of American History* (New York: Charles Scribner's Sons, 1952) p. 65, where he refers to the 'cruelties which follow inevitably from the communist pretension that its elite has taken "the leap from the realm of necessity to the realm of freedom" and is therefore no longer subject to the limitations of nature and history which have hitherto bound the actions of men'.
9. Corliss Lamont, *Humanism as a Philosophy* (New York: Philosophical Library, 1949) p. 34.
10. *Free Inquiry* is the title of a quarterly journal published by the Council for Democratic and Secular Humanism; the issue referred to is vol. 9, no. 2, Spring, 1989.

11. Bertrand Russell, *A History of Western Philosophy* (New York, Simon & Schuster, 1945) p. 364. Though typically whimsical, this view is not without some truth.
12. Lamont, *Humanism as a Philosophy*, p. 75.

2: HUMANISM AS A QUASI-RELIGION

1. Paul Kurtz (ed.), *The Humanist Alternative* (London: Pemberton Books; Buffalo, NY: Prometheus Books, 1973). The essays by Blackham, Hook, Friess, Schneider, Van Praag, Phillips and Williams which are discussed in the text are all to be found in this volume.
2. To avoid misrepresentation, I shall quote the propositions as they appear on pp. 19–21 and thus distinguish them from comments of my own.
3. This is no place to raise this complex theological matter, but if one cites what purports to be relevant evidence, it is imperative that it be correctly understood. According to Lamont, the 'mainstream of Christian thought' has insisted that there will be 'a resurrection of the flesh, the identical body of this world without a hair or a fingernail missing' (p. 118). This, of course, is not so; the idea behind the resurrection image is precisely not 'more of the same' or the unending continuation of what was, but the notion of a *qualitative* difference between what was and what is to be. The point is that we do not have to know what a spiritual 'body' is in order to know that it is *not* a *natural* body that is intended. The philological evidence here is striking. The term 'athanasia', literally 'deathlessness' and translated in the King James Version as 'Immortality' occurs throughout the entire New Testament *only twice*, 1 Cor. 15:53 and 1 Tim. 6:16. By contrast the term '*Aionie*' which means 'eternal', 'everlasting', in relation to God, life and time, occurs dozens of times in the New Testament books. It could be argued that the identification of the Christian doctrine as that of immortality came about as the result of two factors; first, the inclusion in the natural religion as defined by Herbert of Cherbury of immortality on the ground that is supposed to be a doctrine common to a number of religions, and, second, the stress placed on the immortality of the soul by the Deists. The supposition in both cases seems to have been that the idea of immortality is more 'rational' than the notion of 'resurrection'.
4. In the middle of the nineteenth century, scientists working on the relation between energy, heat and work in the field known as thermodynamics coined the term 'entropy' to indicate the fact that as energy is transformed in work it is no longer available as energy. Like many scientific conceptions – Evolution and Relativity are among them – entropy was given a common sense meaning and came to stand for the general idea that the universe is 'running down' with bodies cooling, springs untensing, electrical charges leaking away, etc. A popular rhyme declared 'That no life lives forever; that dead men rise up

never . . .' and even some philosophers began to brood over the possibility that in the end the universe would turn to ice. Bertrand Russell dramatised the idea in his essay, 'A Free Man's Worship', where the free spirit, like Prometheus castigating Zeus, is hurling defiance at the universe in the face of this frozen destiny. Lamont has this idea in mind in what he is claiming here.

5. There are, of course, problems surrounding the use of 'universe', 'cosmos', and 'Nature'. Are they meant to be synonymous? Does any one of these terms include the others? It would appear that 'Nature' is the main focus, since it is the only term capitalised. As we shall see, there are problems with that too since, with the removal of so-called 'supernature' the term 'Nature' no longer has a *contrast* with anything else.

6. Lamont seems to have overlooked the fact that much the same thing could be said about his Humanism; it appropriates for itself all the achievements of human beings and even incorporates the insights of the founders of the world religions.

7. Boston, Beacon Press, 1947.

8. Edited by Paul Kurtz (London, Pemberton Books, 1973; Buffalo, New York: Prometheus Books, 1973).

9. That this is no idle caveat becomes clear when we recall Lamont's claim that it is a 'possibility' that by the year 2000 a world-wide Humanist civilisation would emerge.

10. This term derives from James's *Varieties of Religious Experience* where he used it in a very precise sense to denote beliefs about the nature of the 'More' in religious reality on its farther side that he claims is continuous with the subconscious on its *hither* side. It is clear that what he has in mind is that overbeliefs are those of *particular* religions concerning the 'More', and this is confirmed by his contrast between 'overbeliefs' and 'what is common and generic' to the nature of religion as such. It is not clear whether Hook is using the term in James's sense since it seems to have taken on a life of its own even if it does not appear in most dictionaries.

11. Van Praag was at the time of the writing of his essay President of the International Humanist and Ethical Union and Professor of Philosophy at the University of Utrecht.

12. *Free Inquiry*, 1987/88, vol. 8, no. 1.

13. It is not without significance that in earlier versions, 'Humanism' was generally written with a capital 'H' whereas in the case of the Secular humanists there is a move to the lower case.

3: MARXISM AS A QUASI-RELIGION

1. The recollections, confessions and assessments by these individuals are found in a widely circulated book, *The God that Failed*, edited by Richard Crossman, MP, which appeared in 1949. See pp. 45 ff.

2. One needs to remember that 'economics' as a field of study is now conceived much more narrowly than was the case in Marx's time.

Economics – literally, 'the law or order of the house' – was then taken to include the socio-political, historical situation of nations and of their constituent groups and communities, and not only what we might call today the 'economic' aspect of the situation which usually means how much will a programme cost and where will the funds come from. The distinction is important because it meant that when Marx was writing about 'economics' he was concerned as well with moral considerations, the effect of social arrangements on human life, social and political criticism involving justice and equality and philosophical ideas such as dialectical development in history, the role of *praxis*, and the overcoming of human alienation. Hence, when he insisted on the 'economic' basis of history, he must be understood in the broader sense of the term.

3. *The Logic of Hegel*, Part I of the *Encyclopedia of the Philosophical Sciences*, Translated by William Wallace (Oxford University Press, 2nd edn, 1892) Sec. 81.
4. Ibid., Sec. 119.
5. See Gajo Petrovic, *Marx in the Mid-Twentieth Century* (Garden City, NY: Anchor Books, 1967) p. 73. Petrovic notes that there are some passages in the *German Ideology* which have been used to support the claim that Marx rejected general speculations about man. His reply is: 'But is *German Ideology* Marx's last word in philosophy? Did not he also write *Capital*?'
6. 'The Critique of Hegel's Philosophy of Right', *Karl Marx Early Writings*, trans. and edited by T. B. Bottomore (New York: McGraw-Hill, 1964) p. 52.
7. Ibid., p. 75.
8. *Economic and Philosophical Mss.* (1844) quoted in Fromm, *Marx's Concept of Man*, p. 101. Original in Bottomore, p. 127.
9. Species being – sometimes called 'species life' – is a concept that Marx took over from Feuerbach who used it to define what is peculiar to human consciousness, namely, that we are conscious not only of ourselves as individuals but as members of the human species as well. This consciousness is of a human essence that is the same in all men. For Marx we act in accordance with our nature when we live as *social* beings.
10. Bottomore, 'The Critique of Hegel's Philosophy of Right', pp. 43–4.
11. Because so much has been lumped together under the name of 'Marxism', it is not always easy to find Marx's explicit views. In this case it is important to note that Marx expressly states 'communism' is *not* the final stage in the development he outlines, but only a 'transitory period' in the process whereby a *humanistic* society is to emerge from a class society.
12. It has often been remarked how similar in tone and in righteous indignation over human misery and oppression are Marx's early writings to the judgements on society made by the ancient Hebrew prophets.
13. It is important to take into account the fact that Marx, while he wrote much about communism as the ideal form of political economy, did not think in terms of a regimented Communist Party of the sort that

was developed after the Russian Revolution under the aegis of Lenin and, in later years, Stalin.

14. Richard Crossman, M.P., Ed., *The God that Failed*, New York, Harper, 1949.

15. Crossman, *The God that Failed*, p. 4. The values in which they had lost faith are described as 'Coolidgism in America', 'Baldwinism and Mac-Donaldism in Britain', and 'the collective pacifism of the League of Nations'.

16. The Latin *converto* and its Greek counterpart *epistrepho* connote a *turn away from* a position now seen to be false and *toward* what is now seen to be the truth.

17. Page 34. One can see here how the Party intensified the ideas of both dialectic and the dialectic of history which came from Hegel and through Marx. Belief in the necessity with which the outcome of dialectical struggle comes about in history was the basis of belief in the infallibility of the Party's doctrine.

18. There is a monstrous irony in what Koestler describes; what has become of Marx's idea of alienation and what deeper alienation can there be than this self-imposed deception carried out in the interests of a Party that declares itself to be beyond good and evil?

19. Julia Ching, *Probing China's Soul* (San Francisco: Harper & Row, 1990) p. 130.

20. It is noteworthy that during his incarceration in Spain, the Communist Party did nothing in his behalf.

21. It has often been noted that Communism has invariably found it difficult to find roots in Protestant soil because of the tradition of a revolt in the name of individual conscience against any absolute authority but God.

22. At the time Wright was writing, the accepted term was 'Negro' but since times have changed, I shall use the term 'Black' instead, except, as in the text above, when direct quotations are involved.

23. Letter from Moscow by David Remick, *The New Yorker*, 23 March 1992, p. 72.

4: NATIONALISM AS A QUASI-RELIGION

1. Hayes's classic study is *Essays on Nationalism* (New York: The Macmillan Co., 1926). In view of the widespread acknowledgement of the importance of Hayes's work, it is surprising that his name is not even mentioned in an otherwise good study, *Individualism and Nationalism in American Ideology* by Yehoshua Arieli (Cambridge: Harvard University Press, 1946).

2. The 'artificial' character of nationalism was foreshadowed in Hobbes's theory of the state. Leviathan is not an affair of nature; it is the creature of man through and through and it seems clear that what fascinated Hobbes about this creature is that it represented so colossal an artefact, a machine with highly integrated parts; a monument to

human ingenuity. Hans Kohn also stresses the 'artificial' character of nationalism when he claims that, in opposition to Aristotle's view, nationalism is not a 'harmonious natural growth' stemming from family, village, tribe, etc., but an *abstract* feeling that needs to be made concrete through education, economic interdependence and political and social institutions integrating the masses into a unity that can never be concretely experienced (*The Idea of Nationalism*, New York, The Macmillan Co., 1944, pp. 8–9).

3. The sense of having a *patria* is well-expressed in the poem 'The Man Without a Country' by Edward Everett Hale, 'Breathes there a man with soul so dead, who never to himself hath said, "This is my own, my native land," and whose heart has ne'er within him burned when home his footsteps he has turned from wandering on a foreign strand?'

4. For this special meaning of the term 'nation' see *The Universities of the Middle Ages* by Hastings Rashdall (Oxford, 1895, New Edn, 1936), vol. II, p. 150.

5. Hayes, *Essays*, p. 5.

6. That nationalism does draw on these loyalties if it is to exist at all is not controverted by the fact that the totalitarian state must either crush or reorient the most powerful lesser loyalties that exist within its boundaries in order to maintain sovereign power. One cannot imagine a wider-scale illustration of this point than what is now taking place in the dismantling of the Soviet Union. The Union of 'Soviet Socialist Republics' was achieved in the first place by the bringing together of the constituent nationalist republics through appeals to already existent bonds of loyalty and community – for example, 'pan-Slavism' – and to a common enemy – the capitalism of the West – and then by subordinating all these 'national' interests to the higher power of the Communist cause represented by the supreme Soviet. For a variety of reasons that need not concern us here, this nationalism finally fell apart when it became clear to the people of the constituent republics that their interests were not being represented by nor did they coincide with the aims of the Communist Party and the central bureaucracy. Among other things, this development shows that what I have been calling 'natural' affinities among people can prove to be stronger than the 'artificial' constructions of nationalism.

7. Hayes, *Essays*, p. 24.

8. An excellent case in point is the work of the eminent German philologist, Max Müller, who first developed the theory of an original Aryan language which he identified with race accompanied by the claim that this race is superior to all others.

9. This is nowadays an old-fashioned term coming out of the last century and it is better replaced by clearer concepts such as Otto's idea of the *numinous* or the sense of awe and wonderment in the presence of the Holy, or Tillich's concept of 'ultimate concern' which expresses an absolute commitment to the most worshipful reality.

10. Hayes, *Essays*, p, 102. Consider in this connection John Oakesmith's characterisation of Nationalism; it is, he wrote, 'what the vast majority of civilized people feel to be the most sacred and dominating

inspiration in life'. *Race and Nationality* (New York, 1919). See Hans Kohn, *The Idea of Nationalism*, p. 579, note 2. Kohn claims that this definition holds only for nationalism as it developed after the French Revolution.

11. Much the same sort of ceremonial concern is to be seen in connection with national anthems. Commenting on Haydn's composition of the Austrian national anthem, H. L. Mencken observes that 'When the hymn was first sung on 12 February 1797, it made a colossal success and Haydn became a national idol' (*Baltimore Evening Sun*, 23 November 1916).

12. Jacques Barzun, 'Literature in Liszt's Mind and Work', in *Words on Music*, edited by Jack Sullivan (Athens, Ohio, 1990), p. 211.

13. This transposition shows itself in many ways and examples abound. Many people, for instance, who find it difficult in an age of science to continue to speak of persons as having 'souls' in a traditional religious sense, do not hesitate to make much of the 'soul' of the nation, especially on ceremonial occasions. Similarly, there are those who shrink from the thought of an ultimate human 'destiny' – the 'to Whence' of religious faith – but have no qualms about accepting with enthusiasm the idea that their nation has a special 'destiny' in the course of world history. So powerful was this idea in nineteenth-century America that territorial expansion was placed under the rubric of 'Manifest Destiny', a doctrine which nicely combined at least at that time, clear nationalist aspirations with the typical American reluctance to shed its mantle of innocence by eschewing any show of aggression – the expansion is 'justified' because it has been thrust upon the nation as something ordained.

14. An excellent example is found in the form of an automobile bumper sticker – one of our recent forms of instant communication – which made its appearance at the time of the Gulf War and carried a replica of the American flag with the legend, 'These colors don't run'. The message was clear: to withhold support for armed intervention was tantamount to dishonouring the country and the flag, while marking oneself as a coward at the same time.

15. G. K. Chesterton's ironic comment comes to mind here, although the context is different. Concerning the conflict between science and religion which raged in the last century, he remarked that 'science tells a great many little truths in the interest of a great lie, while religion tells a great many little lies in the interest of a great truth'.

16. Hans Kohn, *The Idea of Nationalism* (New York: The Macmillan Company, 1944), p. 18.

17. Hayes was, of course, writing almost seventy years ago and it is true, as he says, that in the past Islam established common bonds among peoples as far apart as the Arabian Peninsula, India and Africa, but in recent decades the picture has greatly changed. Islam has become invested in some of the most uncompromising nationalisms that have ever existed, witness Iran, Iraq and Pakistan.

18. Page 124. Hans Kohn whose studies of nationalism have greatly enlarged our knowledge of this phenomenon and its effects throughout

the world, puts special emphasis on the *divisiveness* of nationalist aspirations: '. . . the age of nationalism has made the divisions of mankind more pronounced and have spread the consciousness of antagonistic aspirations to wider multitudes of men than ever before.' *Prophets and Peoples: Studies in Nineteenth Century Nationalism* (New York: The Macmillan Company, 1946), p. 4.

'The closer the contact between various cultures and their growing rootedness in the minds and morals of the masses have not only deepened conflicts between nations but have produced cultural tensions which invest the national struggles with the halo of a *semireligious* crusade' (ibid., italics added).

19. This quotation and the preceding one are taken from William James, in John K. Roth (ed.), *The Moral Equivalent of War and Other Essays*, (New York: Harper & Row, 1971).

20. The Macmillan Company, New York, 1946.

21. *The Myth of the State* (New Haven: Yale University Press, 1946), p. 43.

22. Cassirer's treatment of Carlyle's lectures *On Heroes, Hero-Worship and the Heroic in History* is a case in point. Taking note of several writers who sought to hold Carlyle responsible for National Socialism, Cassirer admits that there is 'much truth' in the idea, but hastens to add that Carlyle had no conception of history as a system, but saw it as a panorama of the biographies of great men, and he concludes, 'To read into Carlyle's work, therefore, a definite philosophical construction of the historical process, taken as a whole, or a definite political program is precarious and illusive' (p. 191). It is, however, not clear that Carlyle should be treated with so much generosity in view of the fact that he was rebuked by John Stuart Mill for invoking both human and divine decrees in behalf of Negro slavery and praised by Von Treitschke – a powerful promoter of anti-Semitism in nineteenth-century Germany – as 'the only Briton who had completely understood the Germans'. See Kohn, *Prophets and Peoples*; he cites an article by J. Selwyn Schapiro, 'Thomas Carlyle, Prophet of Fascism', in *The Journal of Modern History* (June, 1941), pp. 97–115.

23. The sentence comes from *On Heroes*, Lect. 11, pp. 41ff, Centenary Edition and is quoted by Cassirer on p. 195.

24. In another of his 'popular' writings, *The Distinguishing Features of the Present Age*, Fichte asks the question, 'Who then in the first place gave to the countries of Modern Europe their present habitable shape . . . ?' and continues, 'History answers the question. It was pious and holy men, who, believing it to be God's will that the timid fugitive of the woods should be elevated to civilized life . . . went forth into the desert wilderness.'

25. This contention is quite absurd. Despite the minority view of some Christian thinkers that 'Jerusalem' should have nothing to do with 'Athens', the dominant position among Christian theologians has been that there can be creative and beneficial interplay between religion and culture. H. Richard Niebuhr's *Christ and Culture* makes this point, but, in any case, Gobineau's claim is totally at variance with recognized historical facts.

26. See Cassirer, pp. 239ff.
27. Ibid., p. 244.
28. See Shlomo Avineri, *Hegel's Theory of the Modern State* (Cambridge: Cambridge University Press, 1972).
29. The movement is not a temporal one since all three co-exist, but it is successive in the sense that an ever-widening community is involved.
30. *Philosophy of Right*, Sec. 340. The full passage of which this well-known statement is the last sentence helps to clarify this somewhat cryptic statement. It is as follows:

> It is as particular entities that states enter into relations with one another. Hence their relations are on the largest scale a maelstrom of external contingency and the inner particularity of passions, private interests and selfish ends, abilities and virtues, vices, force and wrong. All these whirl together, and in their vortex the ethical whole itself, the autonomy of the state, is exposed to contingency. The principles of the national minds (*Volksgeist*) are wholly restricted on account of their particularity, for it is in this particularity that, as existent individuals, they have their objective actuality and self-consciousness. Their deeds and destinies in their reciprocal relations to one another are the dialectic of the finitude of these minds, and out of it arises the universal mind, the mind of the world, free from all restriction, producing itself as that right which exercises its right – and its right is the highest of all – over these finite minds in the 'history of the world which is the world's court of judgment'.

Hegel did not use quotation marks for the final words, but they are taken from Schiller's poem, 'Resignation'. In another place Hegel says that the universal mind is not 'mere might', but the embodiment of reason and hence its judgement is not a matter of 'blind destiny'.
31. *Philosophy of Right*, Sec. 347, Knox trans.

5: RETROSPECTIVE SUMMARY

1. It is interesting to note that, while James thought his philosophy to be as far apart from Hegel's thought as any two thinkers could be, both are at one in their approach to the study of religion. Both wanted religion to speak for itself; James sought to lay hold of religious faith as it is found in the existing individual and Hegel insisted, following Aristotle, that we must follow the lead of the subject matter – what religion in its many forms *shows itself to be* – and not become involved in our own ideas and predilections which are merely private opinions and judgements.

Bibliography

Arieli, Yehoshua, *Individualism and Nationalism in American Ideology* (Cambridge: Harvard University Press, 1946).

Avineri, Shlomo, *Hegel's Theory of the Modern State* (Cambridge: Cambridge University Press, 1972).

Bottomore, T. B. (trans, and ed.), *Karl Marx; Early Writings* (New York, McGraw-Hill, 1964).

Cassirer, Ernst, *The Myth of the State* (New Haven: Yale University Press, 1946).

Ching, Julia, *Probing China's Soul* (San Francisco: Harper & Row, 1990).

Crossman, Richard, MP (ed.), *The God that Failed* (New York: Harper, 1949).

Dewey, John, *A Common Faith* (New Haven: Yale University Press, 1934).

Fichte, J. G., *The Vocation of Man*, trans. William Smith (La Salle, Illinois, The Open Court Publishing Company, 1940).

Hayes, Carlton, J. H., *Essays in Nationalism* (New York: The Macmillan Co., 1926).

Hegel, G. W. F., *The Logic of Hegel*, Part I of the *Encyclopedia of the Philosophical Sciences*, trans. William Wallace (Oxford: Oxford University Press, 2nd edn, 1892).

James, William, *The Moral Equivalent of War and Other Essays*, ed. John K. Roth (New York: Harper & Row, 1971).

———, *The Varieties of Religious Experience: The Works of William James*, intro. by John E. Smith (Cambridge, Mass. and London: Harvard University Press, 1985).

Knox, T. M. (trans.), *Hegel's Philosophy of Right* (Oxford: Clarendon Press, 1942).

Kohn, Hans, *The Idea of Nationalism* (New York: The Macmillan Co., 1944).

———, *Prophets and Peoples: Studies in Nineteenth Century Nationalism* (New York, 1946).

Konvitz, Milton R., *Judaism and the American Idea* (Ithaca and London: Cornell University Press, 1978).

Kurtz, Paul (ed.), *The Humanist Alternative* (London, Pemberton Books; Buffalo, NY, Prometheus Books, 1973).

Lamont, Corliss, *Humanism as a Philosophy* (New York: Philosophical Library, 1949).

144

————, *A Humanist Funeral Service* (Boston: Beacon Press, 1947).

Lea, Homer, *The Valor of Ignorance* (New York and London: Harper & Brothers, 1909).

Niebuhr, H. Richard, *Christ and Culture* (New York: Harper & Brothers, 1951).

Niebuhr, Reinhold, *The Irony of American History* (New York: Charles Scribner's Sons, 1952).

Petrovic, Gajo, *Marx in the Mid-Twentieth Century* (Garden City, NY, Anchor Books, 1967).

Rashdall, Hastings, *The Universities of the Middle Ages* (Oxford: Oxford University Press, 1936; new edn, 1985) 2 vols.

Russell, Bertrand, *A History of Western Philosophy* (New York: Simon & Schuster, 1945).

Steinmetz, S. R., *Die Philosophie des Krieges* (Leipzig: J. A. Barth, 1907).

Sullivan, Jack (ed.), *Words on Music* (Athens: Ohio, 1990).

Tillich, Paul, *Christianity and the Encounter of the World Religions* (New York and London: Columbia University Press, 1963).

Zaehner, R. C., *Concordant Discord: The Interdependence of Faiths* (Oxford: Clarendon Press, 1970).

INDEX